Frontend Development with JavaFX and Kotlin

Peter Späth

Frontend Development with JavaFX and Kotlin

Build State-of-the-Art Kotlin GUI Applications

Apress®

Peter Späth
Leipzig, Sachsen, Germany

ISBN-13 (pbk): 978-1-4842-9716-2   ISBN-13 (electronic): 978-1-4842-9717-9
https://doi.org/10.1007/978-1-4842-9717-9

Managing Director, Apress Media LLC: Welmoed Spahr
Acquisitions Editor: Celestin Suresh John
Development Editor: Laura Berendson
Coordinating Editor: Mark Powers

Cover designed by eStudioCalamar

Cover image by Jerryyaar Designer on Pixabay (www.pixabay.com)

Distributed to the book trade worldwide by Apress Media, LLC, 1 New York Plaza, New York, NY 10004, U.S.A. Phone 1-800-SPRINGER, fax (201) 348-4505, e-mail orders-ny@springer-sbm.com, or visit www.springeronline.com. Apress Media, LLC is a California LLC, and the sole member (owner) is Springer Science + Business Media Finance Inc. (SSBM Finance Inc). SSBM Finance Inc. is a **Delaware** corporation.

For information on translations, please e-mail booktranslations@springernature.com; for reprint, paperback, or audio rights, please e-mail bookpermissions@springernature.com.

Apress titles may be purchased in bulk for academic, corporate, or promotional use. eBook versions and licenses are also available for most titles. For more information, reference our Print and eBook Bulk Sales web page at http://www.apress.com/bulk-sales.

Any source code or other supplementary material referenced by the author in this book is available to readers on GitHub (https://github.com/Apress). For more detailed information, please visit https://www.apress.com/gp/services/source-code.

Paper in this product is recyclable

Contents

About the Author

Peter Späth graduated in 2002 as a physicist and soon afterward became an IT consultant, mainly for Java-related projects. In 2016, he decided to concentrate on writing books on various aspects, but with a main focus on software development. With two books about graphics and sound processing, three books on Android app development, and a couple of books about Java, Jakarta EE, and Kotlin, Peter continues his effort in writing software development-related literature.

About the Technical Reviewer

Massimo Nardone has more than 25 years of experience in security, web and mobile development, cloud, and IT architecture. His true IT passions are security and Android. He has been programming and teaching how to program with Android, Perl, PHP, Java, VB, Python, C/C++, and MySQL for more than 20 years. He holds a Master of Science degree in Computing Science from the University of Salerno, Italy. He has worked as a CISO, CSO, security executive, IoT executive, project manager, software engineer, research engineer, chief security architect, PCI/SCADA auditor, and senior lead IT security/cloud/SCADA architect for many years. His technical skills include security, Android, cloud, Java, MySQL, Drupal, Cobol, Perl, web and mobile development, MongoDB, D3, Joomla, Couchbase, C/C++, WebGL, Python, Pro Rails, Django CMS, Jekyll, Scratch, and more. He worked as visiting lecturer and supervisor for exercises at the Networking Laboratory of the Helsinki University of Technology (Aalto University). He holds four international patents (PKI, SIP, SAML, and Proxy areas). He is currently working for Cognizant as head of cyber security and CISO to help both internally and externally with clients in areas of information and cyber security, like strategy, planning, processes, policies, procedures, governance, awareness, and so forth. In June 2017 he became a permanent member of the ISACA Finland Chapter Board.

Massimo has reviewed more than 45 IT books for different publishing companies and is the coauthor of *Pro Spring Security: Securing Spring Framework 5 and Boot 2-based Java Applications* (Apress, 2019), *Beginning EJB in Java EE 8* (Apress, 2018), *Pro JPA 2 in Java EE 8* (Apress, 2018), and *Pro Android Games* (Apress, 2015).

Introduction

Building elegant and highly responsible, responsive, and stable Java client applications (fat clients) is a highly acceptable approach if security considerations or network availability speaks against web applications, or maintaining servers and server applications lies out of scope for your project. Additionally, using Kotlin as a programming language boosts code expressiveness and maintainability, allowing for a development yielding a clean code approach.

The book introduces JavaFX as a frontend technology and from the very beginning focuses on using Kotlin instead of Java for coding the program artifacts. Many listings and code snippets accompany the text, readily allowing for a hands-on learning style.

The Book's Targeted Audience

The book is for low- to mid-level Java or Kotlin developers with or without JavaFX experience, wishing to learn how to build JavaFX applications with Kotlin.

The readers will in the end be able to use Kotlin as a language for building basic to moderately advanced and elaborated apps targeting JavaFX.

Any experience in using JavaFX and frontend coding is not a requirement for reading the book. Being a Kotlin expert is not necessary either, but having read introductory-level books or studied online resources is surely helpful. The online documentation of Kotlin and JavaFX also provides valuable resources you can use as a reference while reading this book.

Source Code

All source code shown or referred to in this book can be found at github.com/apress/frontend-development-javafx-kotlin.

How to Read This Book

This book should be read sequentially to get the most benefit from it. Of course, you can skip one or the other chapter if you already gained knowledge elsewhere. Taking its introductory nature, the book is not meant to present a reference fully covering each and every aspect of Kotlin frontend programming or JavaFX, so also consulting the online documentation at

https://openjfx.io/
https://openjfx.io/javadoc/19/
https://kotlinlang.org/docs/home.html

while you are reading the book certainly is not a bad idea.

The book is split up into nine chapters. Chapter 1 gives a general introduction and presents hello world-style programs for Gradle, Eclipse, and IntelliJ.

Chapter 2 talks about using properties as data holders and addresses one- and two-way binding techniques for connecting controls and data in your program.

Chapter 3 introduces stages and scenes, which serve as primordial containers for visual artifacts.

Chapter 4 talks about containers and ways to lay out and style your scenes.

Chapter 5 handles nodes and controls including styling. These aspects usually constitute the biggest part of your project work speaking of time budget.

Chapter 6 presents lists and tables, which are particularly important for enterprise-level projects.

Chapter 7 is for summarizing and deepening our knowledge about event handling in JavaFX. This also includes drag and drop procedures.

Chapter 8 introduces effects and animation, improving user experience and giving your programs some eye candies.

As a prospect, Chapter 9 briefly introduces concurrency techniques, giving you a starting point for handling background processing needs.

Getting Started

1

In this chapter, we give a brief introduction to using JavaFX and Kotlin together, and we create "Hello World"–style projects for the command line, for Eclipse, and for IntelliJ IDEA.

Introduction

JavaFX is the dedicated fat client (desktop application) GUI toolkit for current Java releases. It is the replacement and successor of the venerable Java Swing technology. This switch happened around 2010, and since then JavaFX has been constantly improved and extended. With JREs up to version JDK 9, JavaFX was part of the Java distribution—with JDK 11 and later, it has to be installed separately.

The following features describe JavaFX:

- Built-in controls: Labels, editable text fields, buttons, combo boxes, checkboxes, radio buttons, menu bars, scrollbars, accordion, tabs, canvas (for drawing shapes and figures), color picker, pagination, 3D graphics (games, science, product presentation), WebView (presenting and interacting with web contents), dialogs, sliders, spinners, progress bars
- Lists, tables, trees
- Built-in layouts: AnchorPane (anchoring nodes to one of the edges or to the center point), BorderPane (placing nodes at bottom, top, right, left, center), FlowPane (placing nodes consecutively and wrapping at the boundaries), TilePane (same as FlowPane, but with all cells the same size), GridPane (placing nodes in a grid with cell sizes dynamically calculated and on demand spanning several rows and columns), VBox (placing nodes in columns), HBox (placing nodes in rows), StackPane (placing nodes in an overlay fashion)
- Animation (fade, fill, stroke, translate, rotate, scale, . . .), effects (glow, blend, bloom, blur, reflection, sepia, shadow, lighting)
- Nodes stylable via CSS
- Some built-in chart widgets
- Flexible and concise data binding via observable properties
- Descriptive layouting via FXML
- Module support (for JDK 9+)

P. Späth, *Frontend Development with JavaFX and Kotlin*,
https://doi.org/10.1007/978-1-4842-9717-9_1

- Graphics transformations and coordinate systems
- Media APIs
- Java Swing interoperability
- Comes as a set of JAR modules and native libraries
- An external Scene Builder for graphically creating scenes
- Printing API

In this book, we describe a subset of these features, giving you a starting point for your own projects.

Using Kotlin as a programming language instead of Java gives a boost to your coding experience. Just to give you an example, consider a button with a click handler. In Java, you'd write

```
Button btn = new Button();
btn.setText("Say 'Hello World'");
btn.setOnAction(new EventHandler<ActionEvent>() {
    @Override
    public void handle(ActionEvent event) {
        System.out.println("Hello World!");
    }
});
```

(255 characters) The very same code written in Kotlin reads

```
val btn = Button().apply {
    text = "Say 'Hello World'"
    setOnAction { _ ->
        println("Hello World!")
    }
}
```

With 142 characters, this is more than 40% shorter than the Java variant! And besides being shorter, it is also more expressive and by that easier to understand and easier to maintain.

Using some sufficiently nonobtrusive utility functions, this can even be further reduced to 81 characters in size:

```
val btn = Button("Say 'Hello World'") {
    println("Hello World!")
}
```

This works by Kotlin's ability to dynamically add additional constructors to classes.

Gradle for JavaFX and Kotlin

As a build tool, we use Gradle from https://gradle.org/. It is highly flexible, works on any operating system that provides a Java installation, and by means of plugins or preinstalled components can be operated from many IDEs.

I first describe the CLI mode for running Gradle builds. This is how you would use it in a server environment, but it also serves as a good starting point if you want to learn how to use Gradle inside an IDE workflow.

If not already present, get and install a version 17 JDK. Throughout the book, we will be using OpenJDK 17, but if chances are good you can also take Oracle's supported JDK 17 or a higher version from either Oracle or https://openjdk.org/ without any problems possibly coming up.

Note Using Oracle's JDK 17 or higher requires buying a license if you plan to use it for a longer term; see www.oracle.com/java/.

As a next step, fetch Gradle from https://gradle.org. In this book, we use version 7.6 from https:// gradle.org/next-steps/?version=7.6&format=bin. In order to announce Java to Gradle, either make sure `java` and `javac` (with .bat extension on Windows) are in your PATH, or you have the environment variable JAVA_HOME point to your JDK installation folder (recommended). To simplify using Gradle, you can also put GRADLE-INST-DIR/bin (with GRADLE-INST-DIR pointing to your Gradle folder), or GRADLE-INST-DIR\bin for Windows, on the path.

Note In Linux, environment variables like PATH or JAVA_HOME get set via
`export PATH=/bin:/usr/bin:/path/to/my/gradle/bin`.
In Windows, you must use the system settings dialog.

In order to check your Gradle installation, in a terminal enter

```
gradle -version
```

or, if Gradle is not in the path:

```
/path/to/gradle -version       (Linux)
C:\path\to\gradle.bat -version (Windows)
```

The output of the command should be similar to

```
------------------------------------------------------------
Gradle 7.6
------------------------------------------------------------

Build time:   2022-11-25 13:35:10 UTC
Revision:     daece9dbc5b79370cc8e4fd6fe4b2cd400e150a8

Kotlin:       1.7.10
Groovy:       3.0.13
Ant:          Apache Ant(TM) version 1.10.11 compiled on
              July 10 2021
JVM:          17.0.1 (Oracle Corporation 17.0.1+12-39)
OS:           Linux 5.15.0-56-generic amd64
```

Important is the "JVM:" line. The Kotlin version shown does *not* mean you would not be able to build applications running under a different Kotlin version—it just tells it is using Kotlin 1.7.10 for its own purposes.

Next, create a project folder anywhere on your system. For our example project, we call it `HelloWorld`. Change into that folder:

```
cd /path/to/HelloWorld       (Linux)
chdir C:\path\to\HelloWorld  (Windows)
```

In order to initialize the Gradle project, enter (one line)

```
gradle init --dsl groovy --incubating
    --insecure-protocol ALLOW --package book.kotlinfx
    --project-name kotlinfx --test-framework kotlintest
    --type kotlin-application
```

You can also enter just `gradle init`, but then you will subsequently be asked for project coordinates inside the terminal.

The "init" task creates a simple scaffold project which consists of a main project described by file `settings.gradle` and a subproject called "app" in the accordingly named subfolder. The application can be run by just entering either of

```
gradle app:run
gradle run
```

The second variant is possible, because there is just one subproject. By the way, you can list all possible tasks via `gradle tasks` or `gradle tasks --all`, and entering `gradle help` shows more info.

Did you notice that two executable files `gradlew` and `gradlew.bat` and a folder `gradle` were created? This is the *Gradle Wrapper*, and it is a Gradle installation on its own, and you can henceforth use it to build the project. Just use `gradlew` from the wrapper instead of `gradle` from the Gradle distribution. You can even delete the main Gradle installation folder at this time, if you like.

It is now time to add JavaFX to the project. In Gradle, the `build.gradle` file is the main configuration file for the build process. You can find it inside the app subproject inside the `app` folder. Open the file inside a text editor, and inside the `plugins { . . . }` section, add

```
plugins {
    ...
    id 'org.openjfx.javafxplugin' version '0.0.13'
}
```

This plugin adds almost all that is necessary to add JavaFX to a Java or Kotlin project. Kotlin capabilities were already added during `gradle init`. We however still need to make sure that Kotlin compiles for JDK 17 and that JavaFX uses version 19 and allows for using the modules "javafx.controls" and "javafx.graphics". For that aim, add at the end of `build.gradle`

```
compileKotlin {
  kotlinOptions {
    suppressWarnings = true
    jvmTarget = "17"
  }
}
javafx {
  version = "19"
  modules("javafx.controls", "javafx.graphics")
}
```

Note JavaFX is separated into different modules. The modules "javafx.base", "javafx.controls", and "javafx.graphics" are essential to almost any JavaFX application. Because both the controls and the graphics module require the base module, the latter gets implicitly included in any build and can be omitted from the modules list. For more details, see https://openjfx.io/javadoc/19/

In the next section, we code our little "Hello World" JavaFX with Kotlin application.

A HelloWorld Project

The scaffold project built via `gradle init` just prints "Hello World!" on the console if run. As a starter JavaFX project, we instead want to show a little window with a button on it reacting to press events. To do so, replace the contents of

```
app/src/main/kotlin/book/kotlinfx/App.kt
```

by

```kotlin
package book.kotlinfx

import javafx.application.Application
import javafx.event.ActionEvent
import javafx.event.EventHandler
import javafx.scene.Scene
import javafx.scene.control.Button
import javafx.scene.layout.StackPane
import javafx.stage.Stage

fun main(args:Array<String>) {
  Application.launch(HelloWorld::class.java, *args)
}

class HelloWorld : Application() {
  override
  fun start(primaryStage:Stage) {
    primaryStage.title = "Hello World!"
    val btn = Button().apply {
        text = "Say 'Hello World'"
        setOnAction { evnt ->
            println("Hello World!")
        }
    }

    val root = StackPane().apply {
        children.add(btn)
    }

    with(primaryStage) {
        scene = Scene(root, 300.0, 250.0)
        show()
    }
  }
}
```

Save the file. To now run the application, enter

```
./gradlew run     (Linux)
gradlew run       (Windows)
```

See Figure 1-1.

To first compile and build the project is not necessary—Gradle takes care of that if needed.

Setting Up for Eclipse

Note You can skip this section if you don't use Eclipse.

Download and install a recent Eclipse IDE from www.eclipse.org/downloads/. Start Eclipse and then, at Window → Preferences → Java → Installed JREs, register a JDK version 17 and make it the default. See Figure 1-2.

Then, at File → New → Project… → Gradle → Gradle Project, create a new Gradle project. Once asked, enter "kotlinfx" as the project's name; see Figure 1-3.

Keep everything else at its defaults. You end up with a main and a subproject; see Figure 1-4.

The name of the subproject reads "lib." We want to change it to a more meaningful variant.

Figure 1-1   JavaFX HelloWorld Running

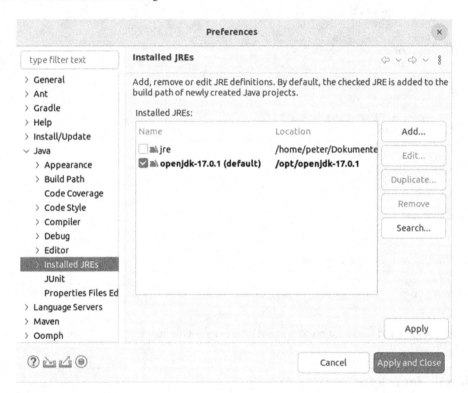

Figure 1-2   Eclipse JRE Setting

Caution Due to a design issue inside the Gradle-Plugin for Eclipse 2022-12, you cannot rename the subproject's name via Mouse-Right → Refactor → Rename… We must apply a workaround.

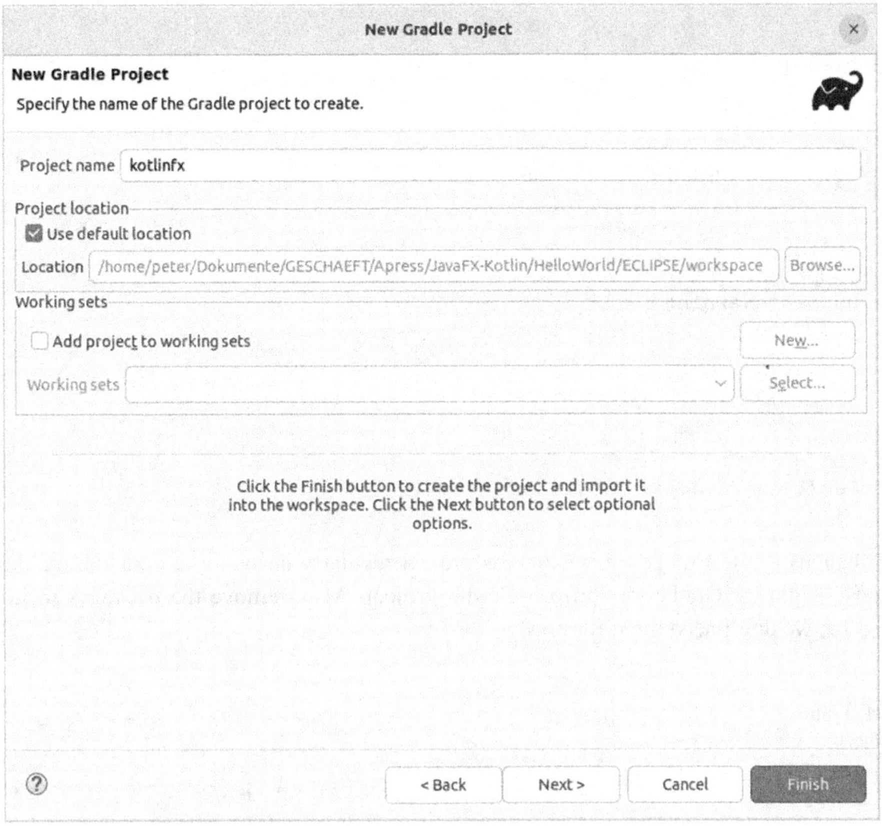

Figure 1-3 Eclipse Gradle Project Wizard

First, edit file `settings.gradle`. Change the line

```
include('lib')
->
include('HelloWorld')
```

Now delete the "lib" subproject from Eclipse. Make sure the "Also delete project contents" checkbox is *not* checked.

In your system's file explorer, rename folder `lib` inside `WORKSPACE/kotlinfx` to `HelloWorld`.

On the main project, invoke Mouse-Right → Configure → Configure and Detect Nested Projects... Press the "Finish" button. Ignore possibly shown errors.

Just to be on the safe side, restart Eclipse. The package view should now be as shown in Figure 1-5.

Back to the application, replace the contents of the `build.gradle` file by

```
plugins {
    id 'org.jetbrains.kotlin.jvm' version '1.7.10'
    id 'application'
    id 'org.openjfx.javafxplugin' version '0.0.13'
}

repositories {
    mavenCentral()
```

```
}

dependencies {
}

application {
    mainClass = 'book.kotlinfx.AppKt'
}

compileKotlin {
    kotlinOptions {
        suppressWarnings = true
        jvmTarget = "17"
    }
}

javafx {
    version = "19"
    modules("javafx.controls", "javafx.graphics")
}
```

After changes to file `build.gradle`, the project regularly needs to be updated: on "kotlinfx," press Mouse-Right → Gradle → Refresh Gradle Project. Also, remove the packages inside `src/test/java`; we don't need them for now.

Figure 1-4 Eclipse
Gradle Project

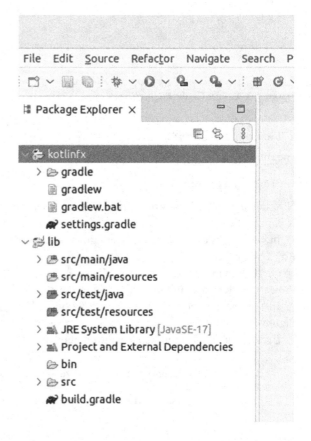

A fresh Eclipse installation doesn't know how to handle Kotlin files. To fix this, open Help → Eclipse Marketplace... Enter "kotlin" in the search field, and select to install "Kotlin Plugin for Eclipse" from the search result list. Restart Eclipse *twice*.

Make a new folder `src/main/kotlin` and register it as a source folder via Mouse-Right → Java Build Path → Source → Add folder... See Figure 1-6.

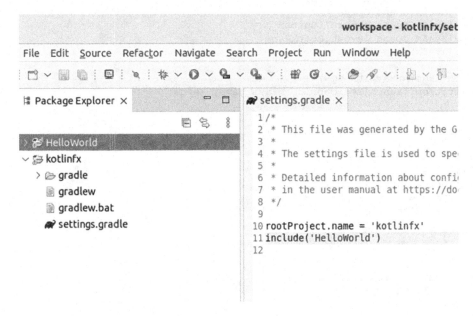

Figure 1-5 Eclipse Subproject Renamed

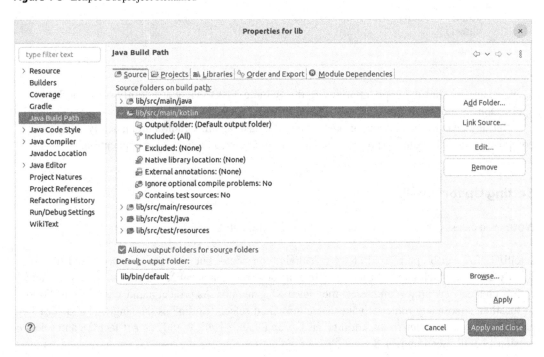

Figure 1-6 Eclipse Kotlin Sources

Inside the Kotlin sources section, add a package `book.kotlinfx` and inside it a Kotlin file `App.kt` with contents:

```kotlin
package book.kotlinfx

import javafx.application.Application
import javafx.event.ActionEvent
import javafx.event.EventHandler
import javafx.scene.Scene
import javafx.scene.control.Button
import javafx.scene.layout.StackPane
import javafx.stage.Stage

fun main(args:Array<String>) {
  Application.launch(HelloWorld::class.java, *args)
}

class HelloWorld : Application() {
  override
  fun start(primaryStage:Stage) {
    primaryStage.title = "Hello World!"
    val btn = Button().apply {
        text = "Say 'Hello World'"
        setOnAction { _ ->
            println("Hello World!")
        }
    }

    val root = StackPane().apply {
        children.add(btn)
    }

    with(primaryStage){
        scene = Scene(root, 300.0, 250.0)
        show()
    }
  }
}
```

You can now start the application inside the "Gradle Tasks" view at kotlinfx → HelloWorld → application → run; see Figure 1-7.

After any changes to the coding, just invoke this task again. Gradle automatically takes care of compilation and rebuilding the project artifacts necessary to run the updated application.

Setting Up for IntelliJ

Note You can skip this section if you don't use IntelliJ IDEA.

IntelliJ IDEA can be purchased at www.jetbrains.com/idea/, but you can also download the community edition, which comes at no cost. To start developing a JavaFX via Kotlin project in IntelliJ IDEA, create a new project and select the "JavaFX" generator. As project name, enter "HelloWorld"; as location, choose any folder at your discretion. Then select "Kotlin" as the language and "Gradle" as the build system, enter "book.kotlinfx" as Group ID and "HelloWorld" as Artifact ID, and select a version 17 JDK. See Figure 1-8.

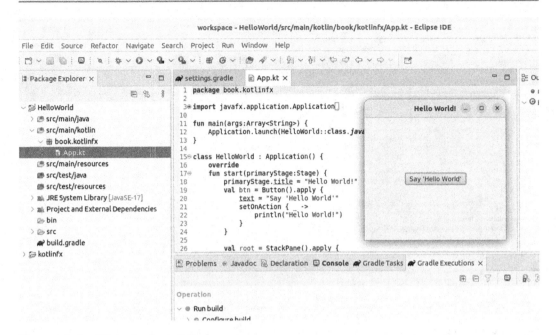

Figure 1-7 JavaFX Application in Eclipse

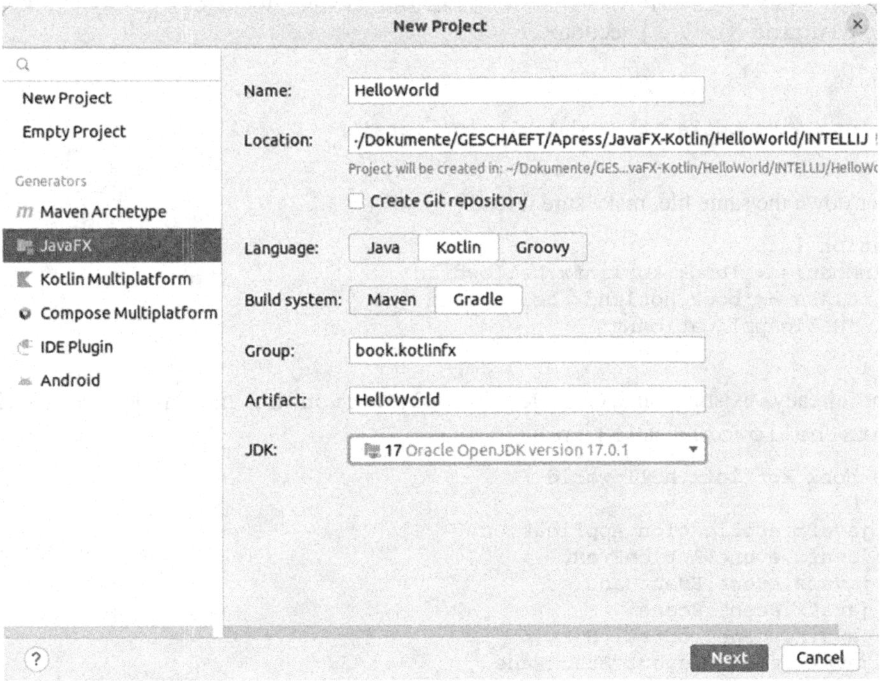

Figure 1-8 JavaFX IntelliJ Project

Figure 1-9 IntelliJ Project View

If you see a classcast exception as shown in Figure 1-9, open the `build.gradle` file and add inside the `plugins { . . . }` section:

```
plugins {
    ...
    id 'org.javamodularity.moduleplugin' version '1.8.12'
}
```

Further down the same file, make sure it reads

```
application {
    mainModule = 'book.kotlinfx.helloworld'
    mainClass = 'book.kotlinfx.helloworld.' +
        'HelloApplicationKt'
}
```

If not already existing, make a `HelloApplication.kt` file inside package `book.kotlinfx.helloworld` and let it read:

```
package book.kotlinfx.helloworld

import javafx.application.Application
import javafx.event.ActionEvent
import javafx.event.EventHandler
import javafx.scene.Scene
import javafx.scene.control.Button
import javafx.scene.layout.StackPane
import javafx.stage.Stage

fun main(args:Array<String>) {
    Application.launch(HelloWorld::class.java, *args)
}

class HelloWorld : Application() {
```

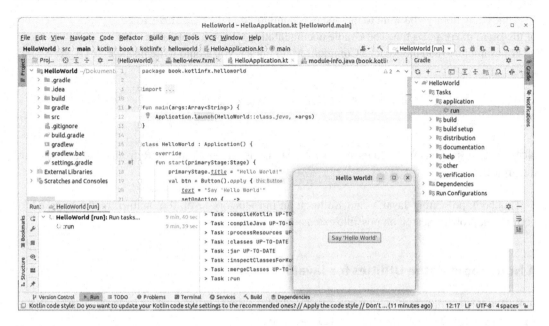

Figure 1-10 IntelliJ Application Running

```
    override
    fun start(primaryStage:Stage) {
        primaryStage.title = "Hello World!"
        val btn = Button().apply {
            text = "Say 'Hello World'"
            setOnAction { _ ->
                println("Hello World!")
            }
        }

        val root = StackPane().apply {
            children.add(btn)
        }

        with(primaryStage){
            scene = Scene(root, 300.0, 250.0)
            show()
        }
    }
}
```

After you open the "Gradle" tab, you can now start the application at HelloWorld → Tasks → application → run. See Figure 1-10.

Kotlin and Java Interoperability

Kotlin sits on top of the JVM (Java Virtual Machine) and as such is designed to access any Java library, including extensions of JavaFX. This way, it is possible to enhance your JavaFX projects in various ways, such as adding math and statistics libraries, XML and JSON processing, networking, cryptography, and what else you might think of.

Almost any library you want to include gets configured in the dependencies { . . . } section of the build.gradle file. The Gradle documentation tells you more about that.

For example, to add the Apache Commons Math library, you would write inside build.gradle:

```
dependencies {
    ...
    implementation 'org.apache.commons:commons-math3:3.6.1'
}
```

Note In Eclipse, you afterward have to invoke Mouse-Right → Grade → Refresh Gradle Project on the project.

This book presenting JavaFX and Kotlin at an introductory level, the inclined reader is asked to perform their own research on possible extensions.

A Note About Kotlin Utilities for JavaFX

In Kotlin, it is possible to write functions and variables outside any class. For example, consider a file src/main/kotlin/book/kotlinfx/aaa.kt:

```
package book.kotlinfx

val msg = "Hello World"

fun abc() {
    println(msg)
}
```

You then can use it from anywhere:

```
package any.package

import book.kotlinfx.msg
import book.kotlinfx.abc
// or: import book.kotlinfx.*

...
    abc()
...
```

Internally, Kotlin generates a class named after the file, class book.kotlinfx.AaaKt.class for the example, and puts such seemingly orphaned variables and functions inside it.

While this comes handy under circumstances, it bears the risk of damaging your object-oriented design. Even worse, you can use such non-class files to add fields and functions to existing classes in a rather uncontrolled manner, thwarting the original purpose of such extended classes and making the code unreadable.

We therefore use such non-class Kotlin files only under the following conditions:

- They do not alter the responsibility of any class.
- There are not too many functions and variables introduced that way.
- They do not represent something that better goes to new classes.

- We don't use them to avoid creating new classes (with new responsibilities).
- We use them to improve readability (comprehensiveness), not to add complexity.
- We don't add more than maybe one or two such files to any project.

Consider the following example: to create a button and add a click handler to it, we have to write

```kotlin
val btn = Button().apply {
    text = "Say 'Hello World'"
    setOnAction { _ ->
        println("Hello World!")
    }
}
```

or

```kotlin
val btn = Button("Say 'Hello World'").apply {
    setOnAction { _ ->
        println("Hello World!")
    }
}
```

Wouldn't it be nice if we had a constructor taking the text *and* the event handler? Even if there is no such constructor defined in JavaFX, it is possible in Kotlin to define such a new constructor. In order to achieve that, we would write in a Kotlin file:

```kotlin
package book.kotlinfx.util
import javafx.scene.control.*

fun Button(label:String,
           action: Button.() -> Unit):Button =
Button(label).apply{
    setOnAction { _ -> action() }
}
```

This could, for example, be placed inside a file `util.kt` (the name doesn't matter), inside package `book.kotlinfx.util`.

For any class, we can now import the extension and use the new constructor:

```kotlin
package what.so.ever

import book.kotlinfx.util.*

...
  val btn = Button("Click on me",{
    println("Clicked")
  })
...
```

Or, because in Kotlin you can write a trailing functional parameter outside the round brackets:

```kotlin
package what.so.ever

import book.kotlinfx.util.*

...
  val btn = Button("Click on me"){
    println("Clicked")
  }
...
```

The little HelloWorld program from the previous section can be rewritten to

```
package book.kotlinfx.helloworld

import javafx.application.Application
import javafx.event.ActionEvent
import javafx.event.EventHandler
import javafx.scene.Scene
import javafx.scene.control.Button
import javafx.scene.layout.StackPane
import javafx.stage.Stage

import book.kotlinfx.util.*

fun main(args:Array<String>) {
    Application.launch(HelloWorld::class.java, *args)
}

class HelloWorld : Application() {
    override
    fun start(primaryStage:Stage) {
        primaryStage.title = "Hello World!"
        val btn = Button("Say 'Hello World'") {
            println("Hello World!")
        }

        val root = StackPane().apply {
            children.add(btn)
        }

        with(primaryStage){
            scene = Scene(root, 300.0, 250.0)
            show()
        }
    }
}
```

Throughout the whole book, we use no-class Kotlin files exactly for such kind of extensions.

A Note About FXML

Around 2012, Oracle introduced FXML, which is an XML-based description language for JavaFX. In order to use it, you must add `javafx.fxml` to the modules list in `build.gradle`:

```
javafx {
    version = "19"
    modules(
        "javafx.controls",
        "javafx.graphics",
        "javafx.fxml")
}
```

In the `start()` method of the application (see, e.g., the HelloWorld example earlier), you would write

```
        primaryStage.title = "Hello World!"

        val location = this::class.java.classLoader
            .getResource("helloworld.fxml")
```

```
    val fxmlLoader = FXMLLoader(location)
    val root = fxmlLoader.load<Pane>()

    with(primaryStage) {
        scene = Scene(root, 300.0, 250.0)
        show()
    }
```

and for src/main/resources/helloworld.fxml:

```
<?xml version="1.0" encoding="UTF-8"?>

<?import java.net.*?>
<?import javafx.geometry.*?>
<?import javafx.scene.control.*?>
<?import javafx.scene.layout.*?>
<?import javafx.scene.text.*?>

<GridPane fx:controller="book.kotlinfx.ch01.MyController"
        xmlns:fx="http://javafx.com/fxml"
        alignment="center" hgap="10" vgap="10">
  <padding>
    <Insets top="25" right="25" bottom="10" left="25"/>
  </padding>
  <HBox spacing="10" alignment="bottom_right"
        GridPane.columnIndex="1" GridPane.rowIndex="2">
    <Button text="Click me"
            onAction="#handleButtonAction"/>
  </HBox>

  <Text fx:id="actiontarget"
        GridPane.columnIndex="1" GridPane.rowIndex="4"/>
</GridPane>
```

Both Button and Text are connected to a controller class book.kotlinfx.ch01.-MyController:

```
class MyController {
  @FXML var actiontarget:Text? = null

  @Suppress("UNUSED_PARAMETER")
    @FXML fun handleButtonAction(event:ActionEvent) {
        actiontarget?.setText("Button pressed")
    }
}
```

Separating logic and design is a valid approach for good practices. So if you like, you can go ahead and use FXML for your project. However, in this book, we don't further apply FXML technologies for the following reasons:

- Coding in a general-purpose programming language like Kotlin, and in a purely descriptive language like XML, imposes some sort of technology breach in a project. While it helps to separate design and logic, bringing those two worlds together sometimes is not that easy.
- XML is static. If you need flexibility for design and layouting, using XML is not the best choice.
- The code in Kotlin often is more expressive and more concise compared to the XML counterpart.

- There is nothing in FXML you can't do with Kotlin. On the other hand, you cannot transcode all programmatic constructs into XML.
- Defining animation or drag and drop operations in pure XML is complicated, if possible at all.

A Note About Downloading JavaFX Releases

JavaFX internally uses a set of operating system–dependent native libraries. Usually, this happens behind the scenes, and you don't have to take care of how this works. Under circumstances however, you might want to have more control over what JavaFX library and native library artifacts get used. To achieve this, download an SDK following the links presented in https://openjfx.io/. After unzipping the archive, the directory, for example, looks like

```
openjfx-19_linux-x64_bin-sdk
    javafx-sdk-19
        legal
        lib
        src.zip
```

In order to use it, inside your `app/build.gradle` build file write

```
javafx {
  sdk = '/path/to/openjfx-19_linux-x64_bin-sdk' +
        '/javafx-sdk-19'
  modules("javafx.controls", "javafx.graphics", ...)
}
```

or for Windows

```
javafx {
  sdk = 'C:\\path\\to\\openjfx-19_win-x64_bin-sdk' +
        '\\javafx-sdk-19'
  modules("javafx.controls", "javafx.graphics", ...)
}
```

So the `sdk` variable must point to the parent folder of the `lib` directory. From here, you can build and run Kotlin JavaFX applications as usual.

Build Setup for This Book

The sources you can download at http://todo **TODO** ENTER LINK consist of three parts:

- An empty Gradle project with each chapter as a subproject. You can use it for experiments and if you prefer to enter the snippets presented in this book one after another. You can operate it via Gradle, but Eclipse `.project` and `.classpath` files have been added, so you can immediately load it as an Eclipse workspace.
- A Gradle project with each chapter as a subproject. Each subproject reflects the state you get after you enter all the code snippets from a chapter. Alternatives that cannot be active at the same time for technical reasons are commented out. You can operate it via Gradle, but again Eclipse `.project` and `.classpath` files have been added, so you can immediately load it as an Eclipse workspace.
- A loose collection of the code snippets from the book.

Properties

2

Properties in JavaFX are data holders with other properties or third parties being able to register some interest in being informed about value changes. This comes handy for user input and output controls in a GUI, where the need for observing value changes and appropriately reacting to such changes is obvious.

In JavaFX, there are following concrete types of properties:

- **SimpleXxxProperty**
  Where "Xxx" stands for one of: Boolean, Integer, Long, Float, Double, String, Object, List, Set, Map. Represents a read/write property. This means value changes propagate to clients like e.g. text fields, but also receives client value updates like e.g. a user entering data into a text field.
- **SimpleStyleableXxxProperty**
  Where "Xxx" stands for one of: Boolean, Integer, Long, Float, Double, String, Object. Represents a read/write property targeting CSS values (node styles).
- **ReadOnlyXxxWrapper**
  Where "Xxx" stands for one of: Boolean, Integer, Long, Float, Double, String, Object, List, Set, Map. Represents a read-only property. This means direct value changes via setters are not possible.

This list shows the more often used classes for including properties in your code. For more information and an exhaustive overview of all property related interfaces and classes see the `javafx.beans.property` package at https://openjfx.io/javadoc/19/javafx.base/javafx/beans/property/package-summary.html or https://docs.oracle.com/javase/8/javafx/api/index.html

All nodes in JavaFX (labels, text fields, checkboxes, sliders, …) use properties to hold data. Via *binding* you can connect node properties to properties in your code. We talk more about bindings below.

Why you Should use Properties

Consider a text field and a button setting the text field's value:

```
package book.kotlinfx.ch02

import book.kotlinfx.util.* // from Ch00_Util
// imports skipped
```

```kotlin
fun main(args:Array<String>) {
    Application.launch(App::class.java, *args)
}

class App : Application() {
    override fun start(primaryStage:Stage) {
        primaryStage.title = "Properties"

        val t = TextField("").apply{
            textProperty().addListener {
                _, oldValue, newValue ->
                println("textfield changed from " +
                    oldValue + " to " + newValue)
                // inform model...
        } }
        val b = Button("Set 42"){
            t.textProperty().value = "42"
        }

        val root = GridPane().apply {
            padding = Insets(5.0)
            hgap = 5.0
            add( t,                     0,0)
            add( b,                     1,0)
        }

        with(primaryStage){
            scene = Scene(root, 300.0, 250.0)
            show()
        }
    }
}
```

The `textProperty().addListener()` method actually asks for a parameter of type `javafx.beans.value.ChangeListener`, but since this class has only one method, the Kotlin compiler knows how to map the lambda construct to an instance of `ChangeListener`.

For the button we used the extension provided in the `util.kt` file, project `Ch00_Util`. In order to use it, you must add a dependency in the project's `build.gradle` file:

```
dependencies {
  implementation project(':Ch00_Util')
  // ...
}
```

The `util.kt` file is listed in the appendix, but it is also included within the book's sources provided as a download.

A text field connected to the model layer of your application design via

```kotlin
val t = TextField("").apply{
    textProperty().addListener { _, oldVal, newVal ->
        // inform model...
} }
```

bears the risk that business logic sneaks into the view classes. For small projects it might be acceptable to ignore this risk, but for larger projects it is preferable to abstract model changes from the frontend controllers. This way we would be able to enforce the separation between the frontend layer and other

layers of the application, promoting a clean application design. For this aim we can use additional
properties in our code:

```
val text1Property = SimpleStringProperty("Some text")
// ...

val text1 = TextField()
// ...

// Somehow connect text1 and text1Property
// ...
```

What is now necessary is a way to connect UI controllers and such additional properties. JavaFX
provides such a connectivity via *bindings*:

```
val text1Property = SimpleStringProperty("Some text")
// ...

val text1 = TextField().apply{
    textProperty().bindBidirectional(text1Property)
}
```

Such additional properties can be moved to an own class, commonly referred-to as *viewmodel*:

```
fun main(args:Array<String>) {
    Application.launch(AppWithViewModel::class.java, *args)
}

class MyViewModel {
    val text1Property = SimpleStringProperty("Some text")
}

class AppWithViewModel : Application() {
    override fun start(primaryStage:Stage) {
        primaryStage.title = "Properties"

        val vm = MyViewModel()

        val text1 = TextField().apply{
            textProperty().bindBidirectional(vm.text1Property) }

        val root = GridPane().apply {
            padding = Insets(5.0)
            hgap = 5.0
            add( text1,              0,0)
        }

        with(primaryStage){
            scene = Scene(root, 300.0, 250.0)
            show()
        }
    }
}
```

Note Such an architecture consisting of UI components talking via binding to properties in a
viewmodel, with the latter being agnostic of UI component classes, gets called MVVM (model-view-
viewmodel - the first *model* represents the business logic).

Another advantage of such a separation is that the viewmodel can be totally agnostic of UI components, greatly improving testability by letting testing code directly access viewmodel classes and their properties.

Inside the viewmodel, you can then add business logic:

```
class MyViewModel {
    val text1Property = SimpleStringProperty("Some text")
        .apply { addListener { _, oldVal, newVal ->
            // business logic...
        } }
}
```

But you can of course factor out business logic and let other classes connect to the viewmodel for that purpose:

```
val vm = ... // somehow fetch MyViewModel
vm.text1Property.addListener { _, oldVal, newVal ->
    // business logic...
}
```

One-Way and Two-Way Bindings

Using properties and bindings makes it astonishingly easy to bind one UI control to another. Consider a slider controlling a circle's radius. All that needs to be done is to bind the slider's valueProperty to the circle's radius property:

```
...
val sl = Slider(0.0,30.0,20.0)
val circ = Circle().apply {
    radiusProperty().bindBidirectional(
        sl.valueProperty())
}

val root = GridPane().apply {
    add( sl,                    0,0)
    add( circ,                  1,0)
}
...
```

Without further notice we thus far used

```
prop1.bindBidirectional(prop2)
```

to connect properties to each other. You might have guessed that there is also an unidirectional binding. In fact there is, and in order to use it you just have to write

```
prop1.bind(prop2) // unidirectional!
```

The main difference between unidirectional and bidirectional binding is, that with the former variant changes from prop1 get propagated to prop2 and *vice versa*, while in prop1.bind(prop2) changes from prop2 get propagated to prop1, but *not* the other way round. This is important for user input controls like text edit fields, which should reflect changes in the underlying property, but must of course propagate user input to the program as well:

```
val text1Property = SimpleStringProperty("Some text")
val text1 = TextField().apply{
    textProperty().bindBidirectional(text1Property)
```

```
}
```

```
// a change in text1Property must propagate to the
// view:
text1Property.set("New text") // shown on UI
```

```
// after user input, the text1Property must have a
// new value (maybe inside a change listener):
val newVal = text1Property.get()
```

For readonly controls like labels, user input is not possible, so an unidirectional binding suffices:

```
val text1Property = SimpleStringProperty("Some text")
val lab1 = Label().apply{
    textProperty().bind(text1Property)
}
```

```
// a change in text1Property must propagate to the
// view:
text1Property.set("New text") // shown on UI
```

So then why not always use bidirectional bindings? First of all, bidirectional bindings sometimes introduce overly complex data flows exhibiting unexpected behavior. Second, in unidirectional bindings you can replace properties by *binding expressions*. For example, what if in

```
...
val sl = Slider(0.0,30.0,20.0)
val circ = Circle().apply {
    radiusProperty().bind(
        sl.valueProperty())
}
...
```

we want to change the slider range to 0.0 ... 100.0, but leaving the circle radius range at 0.0 ... 30.0? For that we obviously need a way to multiply the property by 0.3 This is possible, and actually it is easy:

```
...
val sl = Slider(0.0,100.0,20.0)
val circ = Circle().apply {
    radiusProperty().bind(
        sl.valueProperty().multiply(0.3))
}
...
```

Such expressions like

```
doubleProp.multiply(0.3)
doubleProp.multiply(otherDoubleProp)
doubleProp.add(0.3)
doubleProp.minus(0.3)
doubleProp.divide(0.3)
intProp.multiply(3)
intProp.add(otherIntProp)
stringProp.concat(otherStringProp)
...
```

get called *binding expressions*, and you can use them as a parameter to bind(), provided the type matches. You *cannot* use them for bidirectional bindings, because in a + b c you can recompute c if a or b changes, but in a + b ← c you cannot reliably recompute a and b, if c changes.

The following list shows an overview of all binding expressions. Note that a number property (DoubleProperty, FloatProperty, LongProperty, IntegerProperty) is also an ObservableNumberValue. Any property is an ObservableValue. A StringProperty is an ObservableStringValue. A BooleanProperty is an ObservableBooleanValue.

- **DoubleExpression**
  add(Double | Float | Long | Int | ObservableNumberValue)
      →DoubleExpression
  subtract(Double | Float | Long | Int | ObservableNumberValue)
      →DoubleExpression
  multiply(Double | Float | Long | Int | ObservableNumberValue)
      →DoubleExpression
  divide(Double | Float | Long | Int | ObservableNumberValue)
      →DoubleExpression
  negate()
      →DoubleExpression
  asString(), asString(Format), asString(Locale,Format)
      →StringExpression
  greaterThan(...) (same as add())
      →BooleanExpression
  greaterThanOrEqualTo(...) (same as add())
      →BooleanExpression
  lessThan(...) (same as add())
      →BooleanExpression
  lessThanOrEqualTo(...) (same as add())
      →BooleanExpression
  isEqualTo(Double | Float | Long | Int | ObservableNumberValue, double epsilon)
      →BooleanExpression
  isNotEqualTo(Double | Float | Long | Int | ObservableNumberValue, double epsilon)
      →BooleanExpression
- **FloatExpression**
  add(), subtract(), multiply(), divide()
      Same as for DoubleExpression, but returns
      a FloatExpression if the other operand
      does not correspond to a Double
  negate()
      →FloatExpression
  asString(), greaterThan(), greaterThanOrEqualTo(), lessThan(),
  lessThanOrEqualTo(), isEqualTo(), isNotEqualTo()
      Same as for DoubleExpression
- **LongExpression**
  add(), subtract(), multiply(), divide()
      Same as for DoubleExpression, but returns
      a LongExpression if the other operand does not
      correspond to a Float or Double, in which case
      a FloatExpression or DoubleExpression gets
      returned, respectively.
  negate()

      →LongExpression
asString(), greaterThan(), greaterThanOrEqualTo(), lessThan(),
lessThanOrEqualTo(), isEqualTo(), isNotEqualTo()
> Same as for DoubleExpression, plus variants
> isEqualTo(Int | Long), isNotEqualTo(Int | Long)

– **IntegerExpression**
add(), subtract(), multiply(), divide()
> Same as for DoubleExpression, but returns an
> IntegerExpression if the other operand does not
> correspond to a Long, Float or Double, in which
> case a LongExpression, FloatExpression or
> DoubleExpression gets returned, respectively.

negate()
    →IntegerExpression
asString(), greaterThan(), greaterThanOrEqualTo(),
lessThan(), lessThanOrEqualTo(),
isEqualTo(), isNotEqualTo()
> Same as for LongExpression

– **StringExpression**
concat(ObservableValue)
    →StringExpression
concat(Object)
    →StringExpression, but does not update if the
    parameter operand changes
greaterThan(String | ObservableStringValue)
    →BooleanExpression
greaterThanOrEqualTo(String | ObservableStringValue)
    →BooleanExpression
lessThan(String | ObservableStringValue)
    →BooleanExpression
lessThanOrEqualTo(String | ObservableStringValue)
    →BooleanExpression
isEqualTo(String | ObservableStringValue)
    →BooleanExpression
isNotEqualTo(String | ObservableStringValue)
    →BooleanExpression
isEmpty(), isNotEmpty(), isNull(), isNotNull()
    →BooleanExpression
length()
    →IntegerExpression

– **BooleanExpression**
and(ObservableBooleanValue)
    →BooleanExpression
or(ObservableBooleanValue)
    →BooleanExpression
not()
    →BooleanExpression

asString()
   → StringExpression
isEqualTo(ObservableBooleanValue),
isNotEqualTo(ObservableBooleanValue)
   → BooleanExpression

Custom Bindings

Sometimes the binding expressions described in the previous section do not match our needs. In this case the various static methods from the `Bindings` class (package `javafx.beans.binding`) provide invaluable help. Especially the `createObjectBinding()` method is really powerful and can be used to create almost any binding you might think of.

As an example consider a `Slider` bound to a `DoubleProperty` via bidirectional binding:

```
val prop = SimpleDoubleProperty()
// <- could go to ViewModel
val sl2 = Slider(0.0,30.0,20.0).apply{
    valueProperty().bindBidirectional(prop)
}
```

Because the binding is bidirectional, a change of the property's value would reflect in the slider's elongation and vice versa. The property could also go to a ViewModel, where it can be managed by some data storage, or where other business logic can happen. Back in the view layer, we want the property to connect to a circle, controlling its fill color. This can be accomplished by a *binding* object:

```
val colorBinding:ObservableValue<Color> =
    Bindings.createObjectBinding( { ->
      Color.color(0.0,0.0,0.0+prop.getValue()/30.0)
      }, prop)
```

which finally can be connected to the circle:

```
val circ2 = Circle().apply {
    radiusProperty().set(20.0)
    fillProperty().bind(colorBinding)
}
```

You can see that inside `Bindings.createObjectBinding()` any kind of object can be created. It could just as well be another `Double` object, using some arbitrary formula.

Note The `Bindings` class contains many more static helper functions for various binding creations and calculations. See https://openjfx.io/javadoc/19/javafx.base/javafx/beans/binding/Bindings.html for details.

About Observable Collections

Java and Kotlin collections lack one important feature needed for frontend development: they have no built-in mechanism to tell interested parties about additions, changes, or removal of elements. For this reason JavaFX uses its own collection variants: `ObservableSet`, `ObservableList`, and `ObservableMap`, all inside package `javafx.collections` (module javafx.base).

Such observable collections play a very important role throughout JavaFX. Apart from list views, table views and tree views, there are many more classes that use or return observable collections.

In this section we talk about list views, just to give you some primary insight into how observable collections are used inside JavaFX. At this point we don't investigate such collection related views in a sound fashion, though. This is left for a later chapter.

First we need to know how to create observable collections. If you look at the API documentation of `ObservableSet`, `ObservableList` or `ObservableMap`, you can easily see that these are interfaces. So we feel tempted to look for classes implementing the interfaces. However, there seem to be no obvious candidates for that, so the question arises: how can we get instances of an observable set, list or map? The designers of JavaFX decided to provide a factory class for that. This class is called `FXCollections`, and you can find it in the same package as the interfaces, `javafx.-collections`. The procedure goes as follows:

```
// Creating empty observable collections. String and
// Int as type parameters are only examples - use
// your own.
val s1 = FXCollections.emptyObservableSet<String>()
val l1 = FXCollections.emptyObservableList<String>()
val m1 = FXCollections.emptyObservableMap<Int,String>()

// Creating observable collections given elements.
// Any number of elements of any single type is allowed.
val s2 = FXCollections.observableSet(1,2,3)
val l2 = FXCollections.observableArrayList(1,2,3)

// Creating observable collections given standard
// collections.
val s3 = FXCollections.observableSet(
    mutableSetOf(1,2,3))
val l3 = FXCollections.observableSet(
    mutableListOf(1,2,3))
val m3 = FXCollections.observableMap(
    mutableMapOf(1 to "a", 2 to "b", 3 to "c"))
```

Class `FXCollections` provides many more static factory methods not shown here. For more details see the API documentation at https://openjfx.io/javadoc/17/javafx.base/javafx/collections/FXCollections.html.

Note There are also variants dealing with observable fixed size arrays instead of collections. We don't treat them in this book, but you can learn more about them here: https://openjfx.io/javadoc/17/javafx.base/javafx/collections/ObservableArray.html, https://openjfx.io/javadoc/17/javafx.base/javafx/collections/ObservableFloatArray.html and https://openjfx.io/javadoc/17/javafx.base/javafx/collections/ObservableIntegerArray.html

Given an observable collection, for example an `ObservableList`, it is easy to implement controls like for example a `ListView`:

```
val l = FXCollections.observableArrayList(
    "Apple","Peach","Banana")
val listView = ListView(l)
val btn = Button("Change it"){
    l.set(1, System.currentTimeMillis().toString())
}

val gp = GridPane().apply {
    padding = Insets(5.0)
    hgap = 5.0
    add( listView,              0,0)
```

```
    add( btn,                    0,1)
}
```

```
// add gp to the scene...
```

You can see from this example, that for altering the view contents we don't have to talk to the `ListView` instance. Instead we directly address the observable collection, thus making it easy to extract the view data model to a different application layer, like for example a ViewModel.

In case we want to react to changes in the observable collection, which could for example happen if the user entered data into a view that has been made editable beforehand, we have to install a change listener to the collection. This is not an easy task, because sets, lists and maps behave differently if elements get added, replaced, removed or shuffled around, and we have to take care of several elements changing at once by some operation.

The easiest case is a listener for an observable set. You register it via

```
val os:ObservableSet<Int> = ... // or whatever type
val cl = ... (make a SetChangeListener<Int>)
os.addListener(cl)
```

Since a `SetChangeListener` has a single method interface (SAM = Single Abstract Method), we can also directly use a lambda construct as seen in the following example:

```
val s3 = FXCollections.observableSet(
    mutableSetOf(1,2,3))

s3.addListener { chg:SetChangeListener.Change<out Int> ->
    if (chg.wasAdded()) {
        println("Added to set: " + chg.elementAdded)
    } else if (chg.wasRemoved()) {
        println("Removed from set: " + chg.elementRemoved)
    }
    println("Set after the change: " + chg.set)
}
s3.add(4)
s3.remove(2)
```

You can see that the listener only tells about single elements being added or removed. For bulk operations like `.addAll(...)` the listener simply gets invoked several times.

Just a little more complex are listeners for `ObservableMap` instances. We need to be informed about the addition or removal of key/value pairs, but also about just a value change for a given key:

```
val m3 = FXCollections.observableMap(
    mutableMapOf(1 to "a", 2 to "b", 3 to "c"))

m3.addListener { chg:
        MapChangeListener.Change<out Int,out String> ->
    if (chg.wasRemoved() && chg.wasAdded()) {
      println("Replaced in map: (${chg.key}, "+
            "${chg.valueRemoved} -> ${chg.valueAdded})")
    } else {
      if (chg.wasRemoved()) {
        println("Removed from map: (${chg.key}, "+
            "${chg.valueRemoved})")
      } else if (chg.wasAdded()) {
        println("Added to map: (${chg.key}, "+
            "${chg.valueAdded})")
      }
    }
}
```

```
m3[4] = "d"      // or: m3.put(4,"d")
m3.remove(2)
m3[1] = "x"      // or: m3.put(1,"x")
```

The most important use case of observed collections are observed *lists*. This is because for ListView and TableView nodes what exactly is needed are observable lists to hold the data. Not surprisingly, list change listeners thus are rather elaborated. The current implementation allows for detecting:

- Permutation of elements inside a range.
- Update of elements inside a range.
- Replacement of elements inside a range.
- Removal of elements inside a range.
- Insertion of one or more elements.

Also, contrary to the other listeners described above, the change object provides an iterator you have to loop through to fetch all changes. The following listing shows an example:

```
val l3 = FXCollections.observableList(
    mutableListOf(1,2,3))

l3.addListener( { chg:
        ListChangeListener.Change<out Int> ->
    while (chg.next()) {
      if (chg.wasPermutated()) {
          println("Permutated: " + (chg.from..chg.to-1))
          (chg.from..chg.to-1).forEach{ i ->
              val newIndex = chg.getPermutation(i)
              println("index[${i}] moved "+
                 "to index[${newIndex}]")
          }
      } else if (chg.wasUpdated()) {
          println("Updated: " + (chg.from..chg.to-1))
          println("Updated elements: " + chg.list.
              subList(chg.from, chg.to))
      } else if (chg.wasReplaced()) {
          println("Replaced: " + (chg.from..chg.to-1))
          println("Removed Size: " + chg.removedSize)
          println("Removed List: " + chg.removed)
          println("Added Size: " + chg.addedSize)
          println("Added List: " + chg.addedSubList)
      } else if (chg.wasRemoved()) {
          println("Removed: " + (chg.from..chg.to-1))
          println("Removed Size: " + chg.removedSize)
          println("Removed List: " + chg.removed)
      } else if (chg.wasAdded()) {
          println("Added: " + (chg.from..chg.to-1))
          println("Added Size: " + chg.addedSize)
          println("Added List: " + chg.addedSubList)
      }
    }
})
l3.addAll(4,5,6)
l3.removeAt(2)
```

If you think the fine-grained change listeners for observable collection is an overkill for the task at hand, you can also use *invalidation listeners*. They only tell you, that something has changed in the collection, but don't give further details about what has changed:

```
val l3 = FXCollections.observableList(
    mutableListOf(1,2,3))

l3.addListener { observable: Observable ->
  println(observable::class.toString() +
      " has changed")
}
l3.add(99)
```

We again used the fact that the invalidation listener has only one abstract method. Also, since the code is the same for all collection types, the example shows only the list case.

Summary

Properties in JavaFX are data holders with other properties or third parties being able to register some interest in being informed about value changes.

In JavaFX, there are following concrete types of properties:

- **SimpleXxxProperty**
  Where "Xxx" stands for one of: Boolean, Integer, Long, Float, Double, String, Object, List, Set, Map. Represents a read / write property. This means value changes propagate to clients like e.g. text fields, but also receives client value updates like e.g. a user entering data into a text field.
- **SimpleStyleableXxxProperty**
  Where "Xxx" stands for one of: Boolean, Integer, Long, Float, Double, String, Object. Represents a read / write property targeting CSS values (node styles).
- **ReadOnlyXxxWrapper**
  Where "Xxx" stands for one of: Boolean, Integer, Long, Float, Double, String, Object, List, Set, Map. Represents a read-only property. This means direct value changes via setters are not possible.

All nodes in JavaFX (labels, text fields, checkboxes, sliders, ...) use properties to hold data. Via *binding* you can connect node properties to properties in your code.

A text field connected to the model layer of your application design via

```
val t = TextField("").apply{
    textProperty().addListener { _, oldVal, newVal ->
        // inform model...
} }
```

bears the risk that business logic sneaks into the view classes. For larger projects it is preferable to abstract model changes from the frontend controllers. This way we would be able to enforce the separation between the frontend layer and other layers of the application, promoting a clean application design. For this aim we can use additional properties in our code:

```
val text1Property = SimpleStringProperty("Some text")
// ...

val text1 = TextField().apply{
    textProperty().bindBidirectional(text1Property)
}
```

Such additional properties can be moved to an own class, commonly referred-to as *viewmodel*.

The main difference between unidirectional and bidirectional binding is, that with the former variant changes from one property get propagated to another property and *vice versa*, while in `prop1.bind( prop2 )` changes from `prop2` get propagated to `prop1`, but *not* the other way round. This is important for user input controls like text edit fields, which should reflect changes in the underlying property, but must of course propagate user input to the program as well.

For readonly controls like labels, user input is not possible, so an unidirectional binding suffices.

Bidirectional bindings sometimes introduce overly complex data flows exhibiting unexpected behavior. Also, in unidirectional bindings you can replace properties by *binding expressions*, so you can use them as a parameter to `bind()`, provided the type matches. You *cannot* use them for bidirectional bindings, because in a + b c you can recompute c if a or b changes, but in a + b ←c you cannot reliably recompute a and b, if c changes.

The various static methods from the `Bindings` class (package `javafx.beans.binding`) provide invaluable help for custom binding expressions. Especially the `createObjectBinding()` method is really powerful and can be used to create almost any binding you might think of.

Java and Kotlin collections lack one important feature needed for frontend development: they have no built-in mechanism to tell interested parties about additions, changes, or removal of elements. For this reason JavaFX uses its own collection variants: `ObservableSet`, `ObservableList`, and `ObservableMap`, all inside package `javafx.collections` (module javafx.base).

Apart from list views, table views and tree views, there are many more classes that use or return observable collections.

In order to use them, first we need to know how to create observable collections. The designers of JavaFX decided to provide a factory class for that. This class is called `FXCollections`, and you can find it in the same package as the interfaces, `javafx.collections`.

In case we want to react to changes in the observable collection, which could for example happen if the user entered data into a view that has been made editable beforehand, we have to install a change listener on the collection.

If you think the fine-grained change listeners for observable collection is an overkill for the task at hand, you can also use *invalidation listeners*. They only tell you, that something has changed in the collection, but don't give further details about what has changed.

Stages and Scenes

3

Any GUI toolkit needs a way to communicate with the operating system. It must be possible to detect simultaneously connected monitors and query their size, resolution, and other features, and there must be an interface for opening, closing, and selecting windows. In this chapter, we investigate

- **Screens**
  A screen encapsulates the characteristics of real or virtual visual devices.
- **Stages**
  A stage is a top-level container of JavaFX. Often, but not necessarily always, it corresponds to a window. A *primary stage* gets provided by the operating system, but the application may decide to operate secondary stages as well.
- **Scenes**
  A scene is a virtual construct. It handles visual objects to be shown on a stage, but also introduces concepts like mouse and keyboard events (including drag and drop), a cursor, a camera, and the background color.

About Screens

The `Screen` class (package `javafx.stage`, module `javafx.graphics`) allows us to query some operating system characteristics about the graphics hardware. The following snippet shows how to use it:

```
package book.kotlinfx.ch03

import javafx.application.Application
import javafx.scene.Scene
import javafx.scene.layout.StackPane
import javafx.stage.Stage

import book.kotlinfx.util.*
import javafx.stage.Screen
import javafx.application.Platform
import javafx.geometry.Rectangle2D

fun main(args: Array<String>) {
    Application.launch(App::class.java, *args)
```

© The Author(s), under exclusive license to APress Media, LLC, part of Springer Nature 2023
P. Späth, *Frontend Development with JavaFX and Kotlin*,
https://doi.org/10.1007/978-1-4842-9717-9_3

```
}

class App : Application() {
    override
    fun start(primaryStage: Stage) {
        primaryStage.title = "Stages And Scenes"

        val screenList = Screen.getScreens()
        println("# of Screens: ${screenList.size}")
        screenList.forEach{ scrn ->
            printInfo(scrn)
        }
        Platform.exit()
    }

    fun printInfo( s:Screen ) {
        println("""
            |--------------------------------------------
            |DPI:  ${s.dpi}
            |Screen Bounds: ${info(s.bounds)}
            |Screen Visual Bounds: ${info(s.visualBounds)}
            |Output Scale X: ${s.outputScaleX}
            |Output Scale Y: ${s.outputScaleY}
        """.trimMargin())
    }

    fun info( r:Rectangle2D ):String {
        return String.format(
            "minX=%.2f, minY=%.2f, width=%.2f, height=%.2f",
            r.minX, r.minY, r.width, r.height)
    }
}
```

This shows the resolution, dimension, and recommended scale factor for all screens. The value visualBounds accounts for border regions like task bars and menu bars that cannot be used for windows, because your OS's window manager reserves them.

For example, on my laptop the following gets printed on the console:

```
# of Screens: 1
DPI:  102.0
Screen Bounds: minX=0.00, minY=0.00,
    width=1368.00, height=768.00
Screen Visual Bounds: minX=74.00, minY=27.00,
    width=1294.00, height=741.00
Output Scale X: 1.0
Output Scale Y: 1.0
```

The offset for the visual bounds comes from the menu bar on top and the task bar on the left border of my screen; see Figure 3-1.

Note Although in this example we actually don't produce any visual output, the screen query must happen after the graphics system is initialized, for example, in the start() method.

Figure 3-1 Bounds and Visual Bounds

Using Stages and the Application Class

Stages are containers, where visual things happen. Or, think of an analogy: a theater has one or more stages that serve as physical containers for theater pieces. And, in a theater, the stages don't change if you think of their size and location in the building, unless of course the building undergoes a physical reconstruction, which however doesn't happen too often. Similarly, properties of JavaFX stages are basically read-only properties that can hardly be changed from inside the application.

In addition, in a theater you usually will find a main stage for important pieces. Likewise, there is a *primary* stage in JavaFX, and any JavaFX application inevitably starts with it. It is your decision as an application developer whether or not you want every interaction to happen inside this primary stage or if you need secondary stages as well.

The `Application` class in package `javafx.application` (module `javafx.graphics`) is the dedicated starting point for your GUI application. The approach followed in this book is to create a subclass from `Application` and to override its `start()` method. In the `main()` entry point, you then invoke the static `Application.launch()` method:

```
package ...

import javafx.application.Application
import javafx.event.ActionEvent
import javafx.event.EventHandler
import javafx.scene.Scene
import javafx.scene.control.Button
import javafx.scene.layout.StackPane
import javafx.stage.Stage

import book.kotlinfx.util.* // from Ch00_Util

fun main(args:Array<String>) {
    Application.launch(HelloWorld::class.java, *args)
}

class HelloWorld : Application() {
```

```
    override
    fun start(primaryStage:Stage) {
        primaryStage.title = "Hello World!"

        val btn = Button("Say 'Hello World'"){
            println("Hello World!")
        }

        val root = StackPane().apply {
            children.add(btn)
        }

        with(primaryStage) {
            scene = Scene(root, 300.0, 250.0)
            show()
        }
    }
}
```

The framework calls the `start()` method, passing the primary stage as a method call parameter. The `StackPane` used inside the code only is an example—you can just as well use any other container node. We will handle nodes thoroughly in Chapter 4.

If you need an application initialization procedure, you can also override the `Application`'s `init()` method:

```
class HelloWorld : Application() {
    override
    fun init(primaryStage:Stage) {
        ...
    }

     override
    fun start(primaryStage:Stage) {
        ...
    }
}
```

You must not access any stage or construct any scene from inside `init()`. The graphics framework just is not yet initialized at this point. Instead, you use it for preparational steps like reading data from a file or a database.

If you need to access program startup arguments, you can use the `getParameters()` method inside `init()` (or later):

```
class HelloWorld : Application() {
    override
    fun init(primaryStage:Stage) {
        val args:Application.Parameters = parameters
    println("Named args: "+args.named)
    println("Unnamed args: "+args.unnamed)
        ...
    }
    ...
}
```

Named args get specified as "--arg1=val1 --arg2=val2". Unnamed args are just space-delimited tokens like "flag1 flag2 ...". The sources bundle provided with the book shows you how to define a Gradle task that adds parameters to the application invocation; see `build.gradle` inside the "Ch03_StagesAndScenes" subproject. Also, the documentation presented at https://openjfx.io/

javadoc/17/javafx.graphics/javafx/application/Application.Parameters.html tells you more about the `Parameters` class.

Note We use the same `Application` subclass throughout the book. Unless otherwise noted, any code snippet shown must go to the `start()` method or to a method or class called from inside `start(){ ... }`.

Opening secondary stages (or windows, if you like) is easy. Adding

```
private fun secondaryOwnedStage(primaryStage:Stage) {
    Stage().apply {
        title = "Secondary Owned Stage"
        initOwner(primaryStage)
        scene = Scene(VBox(
            Label("I'm an owned secondary stage"),
            Label("You cannot put me behind my owner"),
            Label("I'm not modal, though")
        ), 300.0, 250.0).customCSS()
        show()
    }
}

private fun secondaryModalStage(primaryStage:Stage) {
    Stage().apply {
        title = "Secondary Modal Stage"
        initOwner(primaryStage)
        initModality(Modality.WINDOW_MODAL)
        scene = Scene(VBox(
            Label("I'm a modal secondary stage"),
            Label("You cannot put me behind my owner")
        ), 300.0, 250.0).customCSS()
        show()
    }
}

private fun secondaryTopStage() {
    Stage().apply {
        title = "Secondary Top-Level Stage"
        scene = Scene(VBox(
            Label("I'm a top-level secondary stage"),
            Label("I'll stay, even if you close the " +
                "primary stage")
        ), 350.0, 250.0).customCSS()
        show()
    }
}

private fun Scene.customCSS():Scene {
    stylesheets.add("css/styles.css")
    return this
}
```

and calling any of the `secondary*()` methods opens such a secondary stage. Common to all of them is the instantiation of a `Stage` object and assigning a `Scene` to it. Opening secondary stages often is a result of user activities on the primary stage, for example, selecting a menu item or clicking a button.

In case you don't know what the `fun Scene.customCSS() : Scene { ... }` is about, this is an *extension function*. It behaves as if you had added a new method `customCSS() : Scene { ... }` to class `Scene`. Here, it loads a stylesheet from the `src/main/resources` folder (the subfolder "css" to be included!) and via `return this` returns the scene itself. The CSS file, for example, reads

```
/* src/main/resources/css/styles.css                */
/* https://www.javadoc.io/doc/org.openjfx/
   javafx-controls/18/javafx.graphics/javafx/scene/
   doc-files/cssref.html                             */
VBox {
     -fx-border-width: 1em;
     -fx-border-color: #0000;
     -fx-spacing: 0.5em;
}
```

and it adds a padding and a children spacing to the `VBox` pane. We'll talk about boxes and styling in Chapter 4.

Dialog-Like Stages

So far, we used the `show()` method to actually force the display of stages:

```
class App : Application() {
    override
    fun start(primaryStage:Stage) {
        primaryStage.title = "..."

        val root = StackPane().apply {
            children.add( ... )
        }

        with(primaryStage){
            scene = Scene(root, 300.0, 250.0)

            show() // <=====
        }
    }
}
```

This method call returns immediately. For standard windows that operate alone or concurrently alongside other windows, this is the expected behavior. Contrary to that, for dialog-like windows a behavior is preferred, where the program flow stops, until the window closes. To avoid having to code complicated state machines with listeners, there is a variant of `show()` making this much easier:

```
        ...
        with(primaryStage){
            scene = Scene(root, 300.0, 250.0)

            showAndWait()
            // fetch user input properties...
        }
        ...
```

The JavaFX Application Thread

Operations targeting UI containers and elements happen inside the *JavaFX Application Thread*. If you ever need to initiate a long-running calculation and at the end update the UI, you

- *Should not* do that in the JavaFX Application Thread, because, while it is running, the UI gets blocked and it cannot respond to user activities.
- *Must not* do all that in a background thread, because updating the UI must happen inside the JavaFX Application Thread. Violating this rule leads to an exception.

As a low-level remedy, you can use the static `runLater()` method of class `Platform` (package `javafx.application`):

```
Thread{
    // ... some long-running operation
    Platform.runLater{
        // ... update/change the UI
    }
}.start()
```

The block inside `runLater()` gets sent to a queue and executed later, as soon as the JavaFX Application Thread finds time to handle it.

This low-level approach lacks lifecycle control, so you cannot be sure the UI is in a consistent state when some other structural activities happen meanwhile. There are also more high-level approaches taking such context-related influences into account. We however postpone this to Chapter 7.

About Scenes

Scenes contain user interface elements and handle layouting and user interaction. While we have learned that stages primarily get controlled by the operating system and apart from opening and closing do not provide much interactivity, the scenes allow us to add visual containers and position elements (controls) of various kinds inside them. You can even move around scenes and associate them with different stages. If you like to go on with the theater analogy, you can consider scenes as, well, *scenes* of an oeuvre to be staged, with a setting, actors, and requisites.

Note There is nothing like a plot though in JavaFX. It is up to the application developer to define interaction patterns and scene transitions.

Not surprisingly, a scene gets described by the `Scene` class (package `javafx.scene`, module `javafx.graphics`). We already used it several times in the book, and a basic coding pattern is

```
package ...
import ...

class App : Application() {
    override
    fun start(primaryStage:Stage) {
        val root = ...
        // <- some pane, with controls added
        with(primaryStage){
            scene = Scene(root, 300.0, 250.0)
            show()
```

```
      }
    }
}
```

With `Stage.setScene( ... )` or `Stage.scene = ...`, we can later change the scene associated with a stage or introduce new stages.

Interacting with scenes is heavily based on using properties. The `Scene` class exhibits quite some methods with many of them returning properties, and in the following paragraphs, I give an introduction to a selection of them.

Position and Size

The following methods tell about the size and position of a scene:

- `heightProperty()` : `ReadOnlyDoubleProperty`
  OR: `getHeight()` : `Double`
  OR: `.height`

  The height of this Scene, as a property, or directly the value
- `widthProperty()` : `ReadOnlyDoubleProperty`
  OR: `getWidth()` : `Double`
  OR: `.width`

  The width of this Scene, as a property, or directly the value
- `xProperty()` : `ReadOnlyDoubleProperty`
  OR: `getX()` : `Double`
  OR: `.x`

  The horizontal location of this Scene on the window, as a property, or directly the value
- `yProperty()` : `ReadOnlyDoubleProperty`
  OR: `getY()` : `Double`
  OR: `.y`

  The vertical location of this Scene on the window, as a property, or directly the value

All position and size properties are read-only. And for none of the values, there is a setter. Usually, there is not much use of the position properties, as they are rather static. You might use the size properties, though, as the following example shows:

```
class SceneProperties : Application() {
  override fun start(primaryStage:Stage) {
    val scene1 = Scene(
      VBox(
        Label("Circle radius = 0.25 * Scene Width"),
        Circle().apply{ radiusProperty().bind(
            scene1.widthProperty().divide(4.0))  }
      )
    ), 400.0, 400.0)

    with(primaryStage) {
      title = "Scene Properties"
      scene = scene1
      show()
    }
```

```
    }
}
```

The circle automatically changes its size, if you change the window width on your desktop.

Camera

Usually, for a 2D setup, there is no camera in use, but it is possible to nevertheless assign a camera to a 2D scene. You can then use the camera's translateX, translateY, rotate, scaleX, and scaleY properties to move the camera around:

- `cameraProperty() : ObjectProperty<Camera>`
  OR: `getCamera():Camera`
  OR: `setCamera(value:Camera)`
  OR: `.camera`

  The camera used for rendering this Scene. Might be `null`

Other than for UI elements, changing an associated camera's properties may happen *outside* the JavaFX Application Thread.

Caution In the 2D world, positions and sizes of elements mostly get calculated by the layouting procedures initiated by panes. Adding a camera introduces a competing coordinate assignment concept, which may lead to unpredictable results.

Cursor

It is possible to define the cursor on a per-scene basis:

- `cursorProperty() : ObjectProperty<Cursor>`
  OR: `getCursor():Cursor`
  OR: `setCursor(value:Cursor)`
  OR: `.cursor`

  The cursor to be used for this Scene

To set a different cursor on a scene, you write something like

```
import javafx.scene.Scene
import javafx.scene.Cursor

scene1 = Scene( ... ).apply {
    cursor = Cursor.HAND
}
```

We will later see how to set the cursor on a per-node basis.

Mnemonic and Accelerators

Mnemonics and accelerators allow to combine keyboard shortcuts with actions to be performed once a key combination gets pressed. The difference between mnemonics and accelerators shows up in the use case of assigning keys to menu actions:

- **Mnemonics**
  Work for *active* menus, that is, the menu or submenu in question must be visible.
- **Accelerators**
  Work for active and inactive menus.

The API for mnemonics reads

- `addMnemoni(m:Mnemonic):Unit`

    Registers the specified mnemonic
- `removeMnemonic(m:Mnemonic):Unit`

    Unregisters the specified mnemonic
- `getMnemonics():`
    `ObservableMap<KeyCombination,ObservableList<Mnemonic»`

    Gets the list of mnemonics for this Scene. Includes the mnemonics that have been added via `addMnemonic()`

In order for mnemonics to work as expected, the event must not have been captured by any node all the way up to the event handler inside the UI's node hierarchy. For example, to add ALT+Q as a mnemonic to a text field, you can write

```
val node = TextField("Press Q+Alt")
val mnemonicKeyCombo =
    KeyCodeCombination(KeyCode.Q, KeyCombination.ALT_DOWN)
val myMnemonic =
    Mnemonic(node, mnemonicKeyCombo)
scene.addEventHandler(ActionEvent.ACTION) {
  actionEvent:ActionEvent ->
      println(actionEvent.toString())
}
scene.addMnemonic(myMnemonic)

... add node to scene ...
```

Adding mnemonics to menus and menu items is such a common task that there is a much easier way to assign keys to menus and menu items: just prepend an underscore to the character you want to be added as a mnemonic. For example:

```
import book.kotlinfx.util.*
...

val menu = Menu("_Menu").apply {
  with(items){
    add(MenuItem("Position & Size"){ ... })
    add(MenuItem("Camera"){ ... })
    add(MenuItem("_Auto Mnemonic"){
        println("Auto Mnemonic") })
  }
```

```
}
... add menu to the UI ...
```

You can now press ALT and then a registered character key ("M" or "A" for the example) to select a menu or to simulate a menu item click.

Caution Both presentation and behavior of menu and menu item mnemonics heavily depend on the operating system in use.

In order to assign keyboard shortcuts to action events on a per-scene basis, you can use *accelerators* instead of mnemonics. The scene class provides the following API to query or register accelerators:

– getAccelerators() : ObservableMap<KeyCombination, Runnable>
  OR: .accelerators

  Access the accelerators registered for this Scene

Use it as in this example:

```
scene.accelerators[KeyCodeCombination(
  KeyCode.R, KeyCombination.ALT_DOWN)] =
    Runnable{ println("Accelerator ALT-R pressed") }
```

The Runnable { ... } is a predefined Kotlin utility function (borrowed from coroutines) you can use to implement the java.util.Runnable interface needed here for the assignment.

Focus

The scene provides two methods you can use to find out which node currently has the focus:

– focusOwnerProperty() : ReadOnlyObjectProperty<Node>
  OR: getFocusOwner()
  OR: .focusOwner

  The scene's current focus owner node

It is not possible to set the focus using the Scene class. Instead, you invoke requestFocus() on a node; see the following section.

Node Lookup

You can avoid creating variables and handing around object references by using CSS selectors and the following Scene method:

– lookup(selector:String) : Node

  Looks for a node within the scene graph based on the specified CSS selector

Instead of writing

```
import book.kotlinfx.util.*
...
val scene = ...
val txt = Text("Some Text")
val vb = VBox(
  txt,
  Button("Update text"){
    txt.text = "Changed!"
  }
)
... add vb to scene, add scene to stage ...
```

you can also use, without having to store the text node in a variable:

```
import book.kotlinfx.util.*
...
val scene = ...
val vb = VBox(
  Text("Some Text").apply{ id = "text1" },
  Button("Update text by node ID lookup"){
    (scene.lookup("#text1") as Text).text = "Changed!"
  }
)
... add vb to scene, add scene to stage ...
```

The obvious downside of this approach is that we have to cast the result of the lookup() call to the precise subclass of Node, losing some type safety.

Snapshots

You can take a snapshot of the visual representation of a scene, allowing for later saving it to a file or otherwise processing the pixel data:

- snapshot(image:WritableImage) : WritableImage

  Takes a snapshot of this scene and returns the rendered image when it is ready. Blocks until the image is taken. You can avoid this by using the other variant; see the following.
- snapshot(Callback<SnapshotResult,Void> callback, WritableImage image) : Unit

  Takes a snapshot of this scene at the next frame and calls the specified callback method when the image is ready. Immediately returns.

The following code takes a snapshot and saves the image in the current working directory (the project folder if you use Gradle to run the application):

```
import book.kotlinfx.util.*
...
val scene = ...
val btn = Button("Take Snapshot"){
  val wi = WritableImage(
      Math.ceil(scene.width).toInt(),
      Math.ceil(scene.height).toInt())
  scene.snapshot({ ssr:SnapshotResult ->
    val bufferedImage:BufferedImage =
```

```
        SwingFXUtils.fromFXImage(ssr.image, null)
     ImageIO.write(bufferedImage, "png",
         File("Snapshot." +
             System.currentTimeMillis() + ".png" ))
     // The block must return 'null', for
     // Java / Kotlin interoperability compliance
   null
   }, wi)
}
... add btn to scene, add scene to stage ...
```

The `SwingFXUtils` class belongs to the "javafx.swing" module that must be registered in `build.gradle`:

```
...
javafx {
  version = "19"
  modules("javafx.controls",
    "javafx.fxml",
    "javafx.graphics",
    "javafx.swing")
}
...
```

Fill and Other Styles

Methods referring to background fill and other scene style settings are

- `fillProperty()` : `ObjectProperty<Paint>`
    OR: `getFill():Paint`
    OR: `setFill(value:Paint)`
    OR: `.fill`

    Access to the background fill of this Scene.
- `getAntiAliasing()` : `SceneAntialiasing`
    OR: `.antiAliasing`

    The SceneAntialiasing for this Scene.
- `effectiveNodeOrientationProperty()` : `ReadOnlyObjectProperty`
  `<NodeOrientation>`
    OR: `getEffectiveNodeOrientation()` : `NodeOrientation`
    OR: `.effectiveNodeOrientation`

    Access to the effective node orientation of a scene. Either left-to-right or right-to-left.
- `nodeOrientationProperty()` : `ObjectProperty<NodeOrientation>`
    OR: `getNodeOrientation()` : `NodeOrientation`
    OR: `setNodeOrientation(orientation:NodeOrientation)`
    OR: `.nodeOrientation`

    Access to the node orientation.
- `getStylesheets()` : `ObservableList<String>`
    OR: `.stylesheets`

    An observable list of string URLs linking to the stylesheets to use with this scene's contents. This is an important method you want to use to add custom styles. For example, `scene.`

`stylesheets.add( "css/styles.css" )` adds the CSS sheet "styles.css" from `src/main/resources/css` to the scene.

- `userAgentStylesheetProperty() : ObjectProperty<String>`
   OR: `getUserAgentStylesheet() : String`
   OR: `setUserAgentStylesheet(url:String)`
   OR: `.userAgentStylesheet`

   Accesses the URL of the user-agent stylesheet that will be used in place of the platform-default user-agent stylesheet

Keyboard

Key pressed, released, and typed events can be handled by the scene. The corresponding API reads

- `onKeyPressedProperty() : ObjectProperty<EventHandler<in KeyEvent»`
   OR: `getOnKeyPressed() : EventHandler<in KeyEvent>`
   OR: `setOnKeyPressed(value:EventHandler<in KeyEvent>)`
   OR: `.onKeyPressed`

   A function to be called when some Node of this Scene has input focus and a key has been pressed
- `onKeyReleasedProperty() : ObjectProperty<EventHandler<in KeyEvent»`
   OR: `getOnKeyReleased() : EventHandler<in KeyEvent>`
   OR: `setOnKeyReleased(value:EventHandler<in KeyEvent>)`
   OR: `.onKeyReleased`

   A function to be called when some Node of this Scene has input focus and a key has been released
- `onKeyTypedProperty() : ObjectProperty<EventHandler<in KeyEvent»`
   OR: `getOnKeyTyped() : EventHandler<in KeyEvent>`
   OR: `setOnKeyTyped(value:EventHandler<in KeyEvent>)`
   OR: `.onKeyTyped`

   A function to be called when some Node of this Scene has input focus and a key has been typed

Caution Key events can only be handled by the scene, if it has not been captured by any path element down the node hierarchy. This means, for example, that a scene key handler can't detect any character key event handled by a `TextField` node.

Setting key handlers is easy in Kotlin, but a pitfall is that lambda expressions cannot handle generics in all cases, so

```
// fine
scene.setOnKeyPressed {
  ke:KeyEvent -> println(ke.toString())
}

// won't compile, because the class implicitly involved,
// EventHandler, is generic
scene.onKeyPressed =
  { ke:KeyEvent -> println(ke.toString()) }

// this however works:
```

```
scene.onKeyPressed = object : EventHandler<KeyEvent> {
  override fun handle(ke:KeyEvent){
      println(ke.toString() }
}
```

An excerpt of the most important fields and methods of the KeyEvent class reads ("static" means a member of the companion object)

- static ANY : EventType<KeyEvent>

    Common supertype for all key event types.
- static CHAR_UNDEFINED : String

    KEY_PRESSED and KEY_RELEASED events which do not map to a valid Unicode character use this for the keyChar value.
- static KEY_PRESSED : EventType<KeyEvent>

    This event occurs when a key has been pressed.
- static KEY_RELEASED : EventType<KeyEvent>

    This event occurs when a key has been released.
- static KEY_TYPED : EventType<KeyEvent>

    This event occurs when a character-generating key was typed (pressed and released).
- static NULL_SOURCE_TARGET : EventTarget

    The constant which represents an unknown event source/target.

- getCharacter() : String

    The Unicode character or sequence of characters associated with the key typed event.
- getCode() : KeyCode

    The key code associated with the key in this key pressed or key released event.
- getEventType() : EventType<KeyEvent>

    Gets the event type of this event.
- getText() : String

    A String describing the key code, such as "HOME," "F1," or "A," for key pressed and key released events.
- isAltDown() : Boolean

    Returns whether or not the Alt modifier is down on this event.
- isControlDown() : Boolean

    Returns whether or not the Control modifier is down on this event.
- isMetaDown() : Boolean

    Returns whether or not the Meta modifier is down on this event.
- isShiftDown() : Boolean

    Returns whether or not the Shift modifier is down on this event.
- isShortcutDown() : Boolean

    Returns whether or not the Shortcut modifier is down on this event.
- consume() : Unit

Marks this event as consumed. The event will then not be transported up the node hierarchy.
- `getTarget() : EventTarget`

Returns the event target of this event.
- `isConsumed() : Boolean`

Indicates whether this event has been consumed by any filter or handler.
- `getSource() : Any`

The object on which the event initially occurred.

As usual, you can use the Kotlin accessor notation, so instead of `getCharacter()` or `isAlt-Down()` you can also write `.character` or `.altDown`, respectively.

Mouse Events

Before we can talk about mouse-related event handlers, we first investigate the most important fields and methods of the `MouseEvent` class ("static" means a member of the companion object).

Note This is just an excerpt—you can see the full documentation at https://openjfx.io/javadoc/19/ javafx.graphics/javafx/scene/input/MouseEvent.html.

- `static ANY : EventType<MouseEvent>`

Common supertype for all mouse event types.
- `static DRAG_DETECTED : EventType<MouseEvent>`

Event delivered to a node that is identified as a source of a dragging gesture.
- `static MOUSE_CLICKED : EventType<MouseEvent>`

A mouse button has been clicked (pressed and released on the same node).
- `static MOUSE_DRAGGED : EventType<MouseEvent>`

The mouse moves with a pressed button.
- `static MOUSE_ENTERED : EventType<MouseEvent>`

The mouse enters a node.
- `static MOUSE_ENTERED_TARGET : EventType<MouseEvent>`

The mouse enters a node.
- `static MOUSE_EXITED : EventType<MouseEvent>`

The mouse exits a node.
- `static MOUSE_EXITED_TARGET : EventType<MouseEvent>`

The mouse exits a node.
- `static MOUSE_MOVED : EventType<MouseEvent>`

The mouse moves within a node and no buttons are pressed.
- `static MOUSE_PRESSED : EventType<MouseEvent>`

A mouse button is pressed.
- `static MOUSE_RELEASED : EventType<MouseEvent>`

A mouse button is released.
- `static NULL_SOURCE_TARGET : EventTarget`

Represents an unknown event source/target.

You can see that most fields refer to possible event types you can get from method `getEvent-Type()`; see the following.

The basic methods to get information about the event type, and to see whether an event refers to a button applied, and to get the event target and source are

- `getEventType() : EventType<in MouseEvent>`

    Gets the event type of this event
- `getButton() : MouseButton`

    Which, if any, of the mouse buttons is responsible for this event
- `getClickCount() : Int`

    Returns the number of mouse clicks associated with this event
- `isPrimaryButtonDown() : Boolean`

    Returns true if the primary button (button 1, usually the left) is currently pressed
- `isSecondaryButtonDown() : Boolean`

    Returns true if the secondary button (button 3, usually the right) is currently pressed
- `isMiddleButtonDown() : Boolean`

    Returns true if the middle button (button 2) is currently pressed
- `isBackButtonDown() : Boolean`

    Returns true if the back button (button 4) is currently pressed
- `isForwardButtonDown() : Boolean`

    Returns true if the forward button (button 5) is currently pressed
- `getTarget() : EventTarget`

    Returns the event target of this event
- `getSource() : Any`

    The object on which the Event initially occurred

Position information relative to the screen, the scene, or the node in question can be retrieved via

- `getSceneX() : Double`

    Horizontal position of the event relative to the origin of the scene
- `getSceneY() : Double`

    Vertical position of the event relative to the origin of the scene
- `getScreenX() : Double`

    Absolute horizontal position of the event
- `getScreenY() : Double`

    Absolute vertical position of the event
- `getX() : Double`

    Horizontal position of the event relative to the origin of the MouseEvent's source
- `getY() : Double`

    Vertical position of the event relative to the origin of the MouseEvent's source
- `getZ() : Double`

    Depth position of the event relative to the origin of the MouseEvent's source

We can determine whether or not some key is pressed while the mouse event occurs:

- `isAltDown() : Boolean`

    Whether or not the Alt modifier is down on this event
- `isControlDown() : Boolean`

    Whether or not the Control modifier is down on this event
- `isMetaDown() : Boolean`

    Whether or not the Meta modifier is down on this event
- `isShiftDown() : Boolean`

    Whether or not the Shift modifier is down on this event
- `isShortcutDown() : Boolean`

    Returns whether or not the host platform common shortcut modifier is down on this event

Two more methods that handle event consumption are

- `consume() : Unit`

    Marks this Event as consumed. The event henceforth won't be transported up the node hierarchy.
- `isConsumed() : Boolean`

    Indicates whether this Event has been consumed by any filter or handler.

As usual, you can use the Kotlin accessor notation, so instead of `getEventType()` or `isAlt-Down()` you can also write `.eventType` or `.altDown`, respectively.

Mouse Event Handling

Mouse button events, as far as the scene is concerned, get handled by the following methods and accessors:

- `onMouseClickedProperty() : ObjectProperty<EventHandler`
  `<in MouseEvent»`
    OR: `getOnMouseClicked() : EventHandler<in MouseEvent>`
    OR: `setOnMouseClicked(value:EventHandler<in MouseEvent>)`
    OR: `.onMouseClicked`

    A function to be called when a mouse button has been clicked (pressed and released) on this Scene
- `onMousePressedProperty() : ObjectProperty<EventHandler`
  `<in MouseEvent»`
    OR: `getOnMousePressed() : EventHandler<in MouseEvent>`
    OR: `setOnMousePressed(value:EventHandler<in MouseEvent>)`
    OR: `.onMousePressed`

A function to be called when a mouse button has been pressed on this Scene

- onMouseReleasedProperty() : ObjectProperty<EventHandler
  <in MouseEvent»
    OR: getOnMouseReleased() : EventHandler<in MouseEvent>
    OR: setOnMouseReleased(value:EventHandler<in MouseEvent>)
    OR: .onMouseReleased

A function to be called when a mouse button has been released on this Scene

It is easy to use these methods in Kotlin. Write something like

```
scene.setOnMouseClicked { me ->
    println(me.toString())
}
```

Note These methods also exist for the Node class. You can add mouse button event listeners on both the scene and any of its nodes, and both receive corresponding events if the button actions happen on the node.

Mouse motion event–related API methods and accessors comprise the mouse entering and exiting the scene and moving over the scene. Their signatures are

- onMouseEnteredProperty() : ObjectProperty<EventHandler
  <in MouseEvent»
    OR: getOnMouseEntered() : EventHandler<in MouseEvent>
    OR: setOnMouseEntered(value:EventHandler<in MouseEvent>)
    OR: .onMouseEntered

A function to be called when a mouse enters this Scene

- onMouseExitedProperty() : ObjectProperty<EventHandler
  <in MouseEvent»
    OR: getOnMouseExited() : EventHandler<in MouseEvent>
    OR: setOnMouseExited(value:EventHandler<in MouseEvent>)
    OR: .onMouseExited

A function to be called when a mouse exits this Scene

- onMouseMovedProperty() : ObjectProperty<EventHandler<in MouseEvent»
    OR: getOnMouseMoved() : EventHandler<in MouseEvent>
    OR: setOnMouseMoved(value:EventHandler<in MouseEvent>)
    OR: .onMouseMoved

A function to be called when a mouse moves over this Scene

Note These methods also exist for the Node class.

A number of drag event handling methods resulting in MouseEvent instances passed to the event receiver read

- onDragDetectedProperty() : ObjectProperty<EventHandler
  <in MouseEvent»
    OR: getOnDragDetected() : EventHandler<in MouseEvent>
    OR: setOnDragDetected(value:EventHandler<in MouseEvent>)
    OR: .onDragDetected

Access to a function to be called when a drag gesture has been detected

- onMouseDraggedProperty() : ObjectProperty<EventHandler<in MouseEvent»
    OR: getOnMouseDragged() : EventHandler<in MouseEvent>
    OR: setOnMouseDragged(value:EventHandler<in MouseEvent>)
    OR: .onMouseDragged

Access to a function to be called when a mouse button is pressed on this Scene and then dragged

Mouse Drag Event Handling

A couple of drag-related event handlers pass over instances of MouseDragEvent that is an extension of MouseEvent:

```
class MouseDragEvent : MouseEvent {
  companion object {
    val ANY : EventType<MouseDragEvent>
    // <- Common supertype for all mouse event types.
    val MOUSE_DRAG_ENTERED : EventType<MouseDragEvent>
    // <- the gesture enters a node.
    val MOUSE_DRAG_ENTERED_TARGET :
            EventType<MouseDragEvent>
    // <- the gesture enters a node.
    val MOUSE_DRAG_EXITED : EventType<MouseDragEvent>
    // <- the gesture exits a node.
    val MOUSE_DRAG_EXITED_TARGET :
            EventType<MouseDragEvent>
    // <- the gesture exits a node.
    val MOUSE_DRAG_OVERMOUSE_DRAG_OVER :
            EventType<MouseDragEvent>
    // <- the gesture progresses within this node.
    val MOUSE_DRAG_RELEASED : EventType<MouseDragEvent>
    // <- the gesture ends (by releasing mouse button)
    //    on this node.
  }

  fun getEventType() : EventType<MouseDragEvent>
    // <- Gets the event type of this event.

  fun getGestureSource() : Any
    // <- the source object of the ongoing gesture.
}
```

(signature only) We talked about the MouseEvent-related event listeners earlier. The MouseDrag-Event basically adds one method, getGestureSource(), that simplifies getting hold of the gesture source once a gesture target gets informed about the event.

There is a well-described distinction between drag-related MouseEvent producing activities and such activities that yield events of type MouseDragEvent. The *simple press-drag-release* activities start with a click-and-hold on a node (the picked node), and as long as the mouse button is not released, MouseEvents get sent to exactly this node. Only if you call startFullDrag() on the scene or node, the *full press-drag-release* mode gets enabled, and the system starts emitting events of type MouseDragEvent also to drag targets. The API related to this event type reads

- startFullDrag() : Unit

    Starts a full press-drag-release gesture with this scene as gesture source. Note there is also a startFullDrag() method in the Node class that you want to use to more precisely define the gesture source.

- onMouseDragEnteredProperty()   :   ObjectProperty<EventHandler<in MouseDragEvent»

    OR: getOnMouseDragEntered() : EventHandler<in MouseDragEvent>
    OR: setOnMouseDragEntered(value:EventHandler<in MouseDragEvent>)
    OR: .onMouseDragEntered

    A full press-drag-release gesture enters this Scene.

- onMouseDragExitedProperty() : ObjectProperty<EventHandler<in Mouse-DragEvent»

    OR: getOnMouseDragExited() : EventHandler<in MouseDragEvent>
    OR: setOnMouseDragExited(value:EventHandler<in MouseDragEvent>)
    OR: .onMouseDragExited

    A full press-drag-release gesture exits this Scene.

- onMouseDragOverProperty()   :   ObjectProperty<EventHandler<in Mouse-DragEvent»

    OR: getOnMouseDragOver() : EventHandler<in MouseDragEvent>
    OR: setOnMouseDragOver(value:EventHandler<in MouseDragEvent>)
    OR: .onMouseDragOver

    A full press-drag-release gesture progresses within this Scene.

- onMouseDragReleasedProperty()   :   ObjectProperty<EventHandler<in MouseDragEvent»

    OR: getOnMouseDragReleased() : EventHandler<in MouseDragEvent>
    OR: setOnMouseDragReleased(value:EventHandler<in MouseDragEvent>)
    OR: .onMouseDragReleased

    A full press-drag-release gesture ends within this Scene.

Note The page at https://openjfx.io/javadoc/19/javafx.graphics/javafx/scene/input/MouseEvent.html gives more insight into drag-related methodologies.

It is easy to use these methods in Kotlin. Write something like

```
scene.setOnMouseDragEntered { mde ->
    println(mde.toString())
}
```

Gestures

If during any drag-detecting event handler you invoke the startDragAndDrop() on the Scene (or Node) instance, the system enters the *drag and drop* mode and starts emitting events of type DragEvent. The API related to this kind of event and the corresponding event handlers abstracts away the physical source of dragging activities, which in most cases is the mouse, and adds data transfer signature capabilities to the drag and drop process. Because of this abstraction, this way of handling drag and drop activities best gets described as *gesture* in the strict sense. There are also other gestures as rotating, swiping, zooming, and so on. We describe those other gestures in the following and first start with the Scene's drag and drop gesture–related API:

- startDragAndDrop(vararg transferModes:TransferMode) : Dragboard

    Confirms a potential drag and drop gesture for this Scene.
- onDragEnteredProperty() : ObjectProperty<EventHandler<in DragEvent»
    OR: getOnDragEntered() : EventHandler<in DragEvent>
    OR: setOnDragEntered(value:EventHandler<in DragEvent>)
    OR: .onDragEntered

    A drag gesture enters this Scene.
- onDragOverProperty() : ObjectProperty<EventHandler<in DragEvent»
    OR: getOnDragOver() : EventHandler<in DragEvent>
    OR: setOnDragOver(value:EventHandler<in DragEvent>)
    OR: .onDragOver

    A drag gesture progresses within this Scene.
- onDragDroppedProperty() : ObjectProperty<EventHandler<in DragEvent»
    OR: getOnDragDropped() : EventHandler<in DragEvent>
    OR: setOnDragDropped(value:EventHandler<in DragEvent>)
    OR: .onDragDropped

    The mouse button is released on this Scene during the drag and drop gesture.
- onDragExitedProperty() : ObjectProperty<EventHandler<in DragEvent»
    OR: getOnDragExited() : EventHandler<in DragEvent>
    OR: setOnDragExited(value:EventHandler<in DragEvent>)
    OR: .onDragExited

    The drag gesture exits this Scene.
- onDragDoneProperty() : ObjectProperty<EventHandler<in DragEvent»
    OR: getOnDragDone() : EventHandler<in DragEvent>
    OR: setOnDragDone(value:EventHandler<in DragEvent>)
    OR: .onDragDone

    Data has been dropped on a drop target.

More information about the classes DragEvent, TransferMode, and DragBoard can be looked up at https://openjfx.io/javadoc/19/javafx.graphics/javafx/scene/package-summary.html.

Note In Chapter 6, we will talk more about drag and drop procedures.

The other gestures—rotation, scrolling, zooming, swiping (up, down, left, right), and touching (pressed, released, moved, stationary)—get handled by

- onRotateProperty() : ObjectProperty<EventHandler<in RotateEvent»
    OR: getOnRotate() : EventHandler<in RotateEvent>
    OR: setOnRotate(value:EventHandler<in RotateEvent>)
    OR: .onRotate

The user performs a rotating action.

- `onRotationStartedProperty() : ObjectProperty<EventHandler<in Rota-teEvent»`
    OR: `getOnRotationStarted() : EventHandler<in RotateEvent>`
    OR: `setOnRotationStarted(value:EventHandler<in RotateEvent>)`
    OR: `.onRotationStarted`

    A rotating gesture is detected.

- `onRotationFinishedProperty() : ObjectProperty<EventHandler<in Ro-tateEvent»`
    OR: `getOnRotationFinished() : EventHandler<in RotateEvent>`
    OR: `setOnRotationFinished(value:EventHandler<in RotateEvent>)`
    OR: `.onRotationFinished`

    A rotating gesture ends.

- `onScrollProperty() : ObjectProperty<EventHandler<in ScrollEvent»`
    OR: `getOnScroll() : EventHandler<in ScrollEvent>`
    OR: `setOnScroll(value:EventHandler<in ScrollEvent>)`
    OR: `.onScroll`

    The user performs a scrolling action.

- `onScrollStartedProperty() : ObjectProperty<EventHandler<in ScrollEvent»`
    OR: `getOnScrollStarted() : EventHandler<in ScrollEvent>`
    OR: `setOnScrollStarted(value:EventHandler<in ScrollEvent>)`
    OR: `.onScrollStarted`

    A scrolling gesture is detected.

- `onScrollFinishedProperty() : ObjectProperty<EventHandler<in ScrollEvent»`
    OR: `getOnScrollFinished() : EventHandler<in ScrollEvent>`
    OR: `setOnScrollFinished(value:EventHandler<in ScrollEvent>)`
    OR: `.onScrollFinished`

    A scrolling gesture ends.

- `onZoomProperty() : ObjectProperty<EventHandler<in ZoomEvent»`
    OR: `getOnZoom() : EventHandler<in ZoomEvent>`
    OR: `setOnZoom(value:EventHandler<in ZoomEvent>)`
    OR: `.onZoom`

    The user performs a zooming action.

- `onZoomStartedProperty() : ObjectProperty<EventHandler<in ZoomEvent»`
    OR: `getOnZoomStarted() : EventHandler<in ZoomEvent>`
    OR: `setOnZoomStarted(value:EventHandler<in ZoomEvent>)`
    OR: `.onZoomStarted`

    A zooming gesture is detected.

- `onZoomFinishedProperty() : ObjectProperty<EventHandler<in ZoomEvent»`
    OR: `getOnZoomFinished() : EventHandler<in ZoomEvent>`
    OR: `setOnZoomFinished(value:EventHandler<in ZoomEvent>)`
    OR: `.onZoomFinished`

A zooming gesture ends.

- onSwipeDownProperty() : ObjectProperty<EventHandler<in SwipeEvent»
    OR: getOnSwipeDown() : EventHandler<in SwipeEvent>
    OR: setOnSwipeDown(value:EventHandler<in SwipeEvent>)
    OR: .onSwipeDown

    A downward swipe gesture happens in this scene.

- onSwipeUpProperty() : ObjectProperty<EventHandler<in SwipeEvent»
    OR: getOnSwipeUp() : EventHandler<in SwipeEvent>
    OR: setOnSwipeUp(value:EventHandler<in SwipeEvent>)
    OR: .onSwipeUp

    An upward swipe gesture happens in this scene.

- onSwipeLeftProperty() : ObjectProperty<EventHandler<in SwipeEvent»
    OR: getOnSwipeLeft() : EventHandler<in SwipeEvent>
    OR: setOnSwipeLeft(value:EventHandler<in SwipeEvent>)
    OR: .onSwipeLeft

    A leftward swipe gesture happens in this scene.

- onSwipeRightProperty() : ObjectProperty<EventHandler<in SwipeEvent»
    OR: getOnSwipeRight() : EventHandler<in SwipeEvent>
    OR: setOnSwipeRight(value:EventHandler<in SwipeEvent>)
    OR: .onSwipeRight

    A rightward swipe gesture happens in this scene.

- onTouchPressedProperty() : ObjectProperty<EventHandler
  <in TouchEvent»
    OR: getOnTouchPressed() : EventHandler<in TouchEvent>
    OR: setOnTouchPressed(value:EventHandler<in TouchEvent>)
    OR: .onTouchPressed

    A new touch point is pressed.

- onTouchMovedProperty() : ObjectProperty<EventHandler<in TouchEvent»
    OR: getOnTouchMoved() : EventHandler<in TouchEvent>
    OR: setOnTouchMoved(value:EventHandler<in TouchEvent>)
    OR: .onTouchMoved

    A touch point is moved.

- onTouchStationaryProperty() : ObjectProperty<EventHandler
  <in TouchEvent»
    OR: getOnTouchStationary() : EventHandler<in TouchEvent>
    OR: setOnTouchStationary(value:EventHandler<in TouchEvent>)
    OR: .onTouchStationary

    A touch point stays pressed and still.

- onTouchReleasedProperty() : ObjectProperty<EventHandler
  <in TouchEvent»
    OR: getOnTouchReleased() : EventHandler<in TouchEvent>
    OR: setOnTouchReleased(value:EventHandler<in TouchEvent>)
    OR: .onTouchReleased

    A touch point is released.

More information about the classes `RotateEvent`, `ScrollEvent`, `ZoomEvent`, `Swipe Event`, and `TouchEvent` can be looked up at https://openjfx.io/javadoc/19/javafx.graphics/javafx/scene/package-summary.html.

It is easy to use these methods in Kotlin. Write something like

```
scene.setOnDragEntered { de ->
    println(mde.toString())
}
```

Summary

In this chapter, we investigated screens, stages, and scenes, identifying them as top-level containers for GUI elements. While screens strongly correlate to hardware components as displays, and stages primarily represent windows and other more static properties of a GUI environment, scenes are places where one would position controllers and other GUI elements.

We have seen how stages and scenes cooperate and how we can bootstrap a JavaFX application using Kotlin as a programming language.

Furthermore, we learned about the plethora of properties the `Scene` class has to offer, including event handlers: position and size, camera, cursor, mnemonics and accelerators, focus, node lookup via CSS selectors, snapshots, fill and other styles, keyboard, mouse events, and gestures.

Containers

4

GUI elements in JavaFX are ordered in a hierarchical tree-like fashion on a scene. The bottommost element is called the root element or root *node*, and in the majority of cases, this will be a container node (or pane), comprising child nodes that can be container nodes in turn, or leaf nodes that represent purely graphical elements like texts or images, and controller nodes like text input fields, buttons, sliders, or other.

The UI elements all get called nodes, but for clarity we sometimes name container nodes just *containers* or *panes*. If we talk of a *control*, we mean a node the user can interact with. The latter also includes control panes, that is, panes which provide some kind of controllability like scrolling, switching, and so on. An excerpt of the class hierarchy is shown in Figure 4-1.

In our very first JavaFX application

```kotlin
package book.kotlinfx

import javafx.application.Application
import javafx.event.ActionEvent
import javafx.event.EventHandler
import javafx.scene.Scene
import javafx.scene.control.Button
import javafx.scene.layout.StackPane
import javafx.stage.Stage

fun main(args:Array<String>) {
    Application.launch(HelloWorld::class.java, *args)
}

class HelloWorld : Application() {
    override
    fun start(primaryStage:Stage) {
        primaryStage.title = "Hello World!"
        val btn = Button().apply {
            text = "Say 'Hello World'"
            setOnAction { evnt ->
                println("Hello World!")
            }
        }

        val root = StackPane().apply {
            children.add(btn)
        }
```

P. Späth, *Frontend Development with JavaFX and Kotlin*,
https://doi.org/10.1007/978-1-4842-9717-9_4

```
            with(primaryStage){
                scene = Scene(root, 300.0, 250.0)
                show()
            }
        }
    }
```

more precisely in

```
    fun start(primaryStage:Stage) {

        val root = StackPane().apply {
            ...
        }

        with(primaryStage){
            scene = Scene(root, 300.0, 250.0)
            show()
        }
    }
```

we defined a *root node* named "root" and via

```
    primaryStage.scene = Scene(root, ...)
```

(this is what `with ( ... ){ ... }` does) we added it to the scene and in turn added the scene to the primary stage.

The `StackPane` used here is a *pane* (or container) with a very simple idea of how to position its child nodes. In fact, without further precautions, it centers them or just assigns to them a (0, 0) as coordinates, irrespective of whether or not they overlap, which is fine for a simple example.

For layouts using other types of containers, the idea is still the same. You write

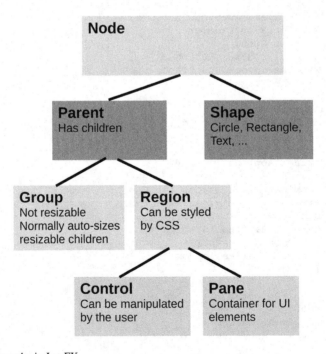

Figure 4-1 Node Hierarchy in JavaFX

```
fun start(primaryStage:Stage) {
    val root = SomePaneClass(...).apply {
        children.addAll( ..., ..., ... )
        // (add children)
    }

    with(primaryStage){
        scene = Scene(root, 300.0, 250.0)
        show()
    }
}
```

and substitute any concrete pane class for "SomePaneClass."

JavaFX contains a number of pane implementations that can all be found in package javafx.scene.layout (module javafx.graphics):

– **StackPane**
  Lays out its children in a back-to-front stack and tries to resize each child to fill the pane's complete content area, effectively placing all resizable children at $(0, 0)$. Nonresizable children by default get centered. This implies that children may overlap.
– **VBox**
  Lays out its children in a single column.
– **HBox**
  Lays out its children in a single row.
– **FlowPane**
  Lays out its children in rows, wrapping at the pane's right boundary.
– **GridPane**
  Lays out its children in a grid, dynamically adjusting each column's width and each row's height. A cell may span over several rows and columns.
– **TilePane**
  Lays out its children in a grid of uniformly sized tiles.
– **BorderPane**
  Lays out children in top, left, right, bottom, and center positions. Top and button nodes get stretched to the pane's full width, left and right nodes get stretched vertically, but limited to the remaining vertical space, and the center node gets all that is left.
– **AnchorPane**
  Lays out children by constraints describing distances from a child's edge to the corresponding pane's edge.

This list does not include control panes, which are described in Chapter 5.

It is also possible to create your own pane classes, but this is out of scope for this book. However, the predefined pane classes encompass the majority of possible layouting needs, so in the following paragraphs we examine each of them more thoroughly.

StackPane

A StackPane puts its children on a stack, paints them in FIFO order (first in first out, or back-to-top), and positions them independently of each other.

In order to add children to a StackPane, either use the constructor or its `children` property:

```
val root = StackPane(node1, node2, ...)

// or

val root = StackPane().apply {
  with(children){
      add(node1)
      add(node2)
      ...
}}

// or

val root = StackPane().apply {
  children.addAll(
      node1,
      node2,
      ...
  )}
```

During layouting, the StackPane first tries to resize each child to the size of the pane, unless it cannot be resized or its maximum dimension, set via `maxWidth` and `maxHeight` (properties of the `Region` class), prevents it from being expanded. If a child is too small and cannot fully be expanded, it by default will be positioned at the center of the pane. If you want to override this behavior and position a small child at a different location, you can do so as follows:

```
val root = StackPane()
val txt = Text("Bottom Right+") // cannot be resized

// tell where to put the child
StackPane.setAlignment(txt, Pos.BOTTOM_RIGHT)

// add some margin, effectively shifting the child
// away from the edge or corner:
StackPane.setMargin(txt, Insets(0.0, 10.0, 10.0, 0.0))

root.children.add(txt)
```

Here, the `Pos` class allows for the following positions (excerpt, only relevant constants shown):

- **BOTTOM_CENTER**
  On the bottom vertically and on the center horizontally
- **BOTTOM_LEFT**
  On the bottom vertically and on the left horizontally
- **BOTTOM_RIGHT**
  On the bottom vertically and on the right horizontally
- **CENTER**
  On the center both vertically and horizontally
- **CENTER_LEFT**
  On the center vertically and on the left horizontally
- **CENTER_RIGHT**
  On the center vertically and on the right horizontally
- **TOP_CENTER**
  On the top vertically and on the center horizontally

– **TOP_LEFT**
  On the top vertically and on the left horizontally
– **TOP_RIGHT**
  On the top vertically and on the right horizontally

In relation to its parent, a StackPane gets sized as follows: Its minimum width and height get set to the largest minimum width or height of all of its children (plus insets, if applicable). Its preferred width and height get set to the largest preferred width or height of all of its children (plus insets, if applicable). And its maximum width and height get set unbound.

VBox and HBox

VBox'es and HBox'es lay out their children in a single column or row, respectively. VBox'es try to resize their children to their preferred height, and they try to resize them to the pane's width, unless you set `fillWidth` to false, which, if possible, stretches them to their preferred width. HBox'es in turn try to resize their children to their preferred width, and they try to resize them to the pane's height, unless you set `fillHeight` to false, which, if possible, stretches them to their preferred height. For both VBox'es and HBox'es, children that cannot fully be stretched, by default, get aligned at `Pos.TOP_LEFT`. You can change the latter via the `alignment` property.

A layout built on a hierarchy of VBox'es and HBox'es usually leads to an alternation of those types, as the following example shows:

```
val root =
  VBox(
    Text("Some Text"),
    Circle(60.0, Color.LIGHTGREEN),
    HBox(
      Text("Some Text"),
      VBox(
        Button("Some Button"),
        Text("Some Text")
      )
    )
  )
```

The output of this example is shown in Figure 4-2 (some additional colorings have been added for illustration purposes, and the menu is not shown in the code).

If the VBox or HBox itself gets stretched by its parent beyond its own preferred size, the extra space by default is left unused. If you want to change this behavior, you can ask one child to use up that extra space:

```
val hbox = HBox()
val tf = TextField()

HBox.setHgrow(tf, Priority.ALWAYS)
// for a VBox use VBox.setVgrow()

hbox.children.addAll(..., tf, ...)
```

If you do that for several children, the extra space gets evenly distributed among them.

Figure 4-2 Node
Hierarchy in JavaFX

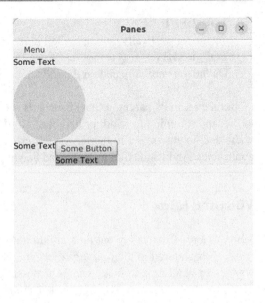

With respect to its parent, a VBox's minimum (/preferred) height is the sum of all children's minimum (/preferred) height plus spacing plus insets. An HBox's minimum (/preferred) width is the sum of all children's minimum (/preferred) width plus spacing plus insets. A VBox's minimum (/preferred) width is the largest of all children's minimum (/preferred) width plus spacing plus insets. An HBox's minimum (/preferred) height is the largest of all children's minimum (/preferred) height plus spacing plus insets. For both HBox'es and VBox'es, the maximum size is unbound.

In order to set a margin to individual VBox or HBox children, or to set a spacing between all the children, write as follows:

```
val hbox = HBox()
val tf = TextField() // just an example
HBox.setMargin(tf, Insets(20.0,10.0,20.0,10.0))

hbox.spacing = 0.5
// You can also do that in the constructor:
//    val hbox = HBox(0.5)

hbox.children.add(tf)


val vbox = VBox()
val btn = Button("Click Me") // just an example
VBox.setMargin(btn, Insets(20.0,10.0,20.0,10.0))

vbox.spacing = 0.5
// You can also do that in the constructor:
//    val vbox = VBox(0.5)

vbox.children.add(btn)
```

For both VBox and HBox, there are also constructors for specifying a gap and all children at once:

```
val hbox = HBox(5.0,
    Text("Text1"),
    Text("Text1"),
    ... )
```

```
val vbox = VBox(5.0,
    Text("Text1"),
    Text("Text1"),
    ... )
```

FlowPane

A FlowPane lays out its children like words on a sheet of paper, from left to right, wrapping at the pane's boundary. As a variant, the flow may also happen top-to-bottom, wrapping at the bottom edge.

The FlowPane's `prefWrapLength` must be set to define the FlowPane's preferred width (or height, if the orientation is vertical):

```
val fp = FlowPane().apply {
    prefWrapLength = 500.0
}
```

If you don't set it, the default value 400.0 will be taken instead.

If you instead want a right-to-left flow, you can adjust the FlowPane as follows:

```
val fp = FlowPane().apply {
    prefWrapLength = 500.0
    nodeOrientation = NodeOrientation.RIGHT_TO_LEFT
    // Wrapping at the left edge
}
```

The orientation can be provided in the constructor, or you can later set it as a property:

```
val fp = FlowPane()
// The default is left-to-right, and wrapping at the
// right edge. prefWrapLength = 400.0

val fp2 = FlowPane(Orientation.VERTICAL)
// Top-to-bottom, and wrapping at the bottom edge.
// prefWrapLength = 400.0

fp.orientation = Orientation.VERTICAL
// Setting via property
```

An example for using a FlowPane reads

```
package book.kotlinfx.ch04

fun main(args: Array<String>) {
    Application.launch(App::class.java, *args)
}

class App : Application() {
    override
    fun start(primaryStage: Stage) {
        primaryStage.title = "FlowPane"

        val root = FlowPane()
        (1..20).forEach { i ->
          fp.children.add(
            Button("${i}").apply{
               prefWidth = 40.0 + 50.0 * Math.random()   }
            )
```

```
        }

    root.children.add( VBox(5.0,
        HBox(5.0,
            CheckBox("Right-to-Left").apply{
                setOnAction {
                    if(isSelected) {
                        fp.nodeOrientation =
                            NodeOrientation.RIGHT_TO_LEFT
                    }else{
                        fp.nodeOrientation =
                            NodeOrientation.LEFT_TO_RIGHT
                    }
                }
            },
            CheckBox("Vertical").apply{
                setOnAction {
                    if(isSelected) {
                        fp.orientation =
                            Orientation.VERTICAL
                    }else{
                        fp.orientation =
                            Orientation.HORIZONTAL
                    }
                }
            }
        ),
        fp
    ) )
    with(primaryStage) {
        scene = Scene(root, 400.0, 350.0).customCSS()
        show()
    }
}

private fun Scene.customCSS():Scene {
    stylesheets.add("css/styles.css")
    return this
}
}
```

(imports not shown) It allows for setting the flow direction (left-to-right or right-to-left) and the orientation (horizontal or vertical). File `styles.css` sets some basic styles. It must go to `src/main/resources/css` and reads

```
VBox {
  -fx-border-width: 1em;
  -fx-border-color: #0000;
  -fx-spacing: 0.5em;
}
```

We talk more about styling later in the book.

The outcome of this example is shown in Figure 4-3.

Figure 4-3 A FlowPane

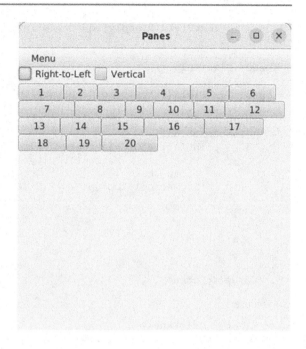

GridPane

A GridPane lays out its children in a grid with flexible, by default, automatically computed column widths and row heights. The children may be freely placed on any row and column, and it may span multiple rows and columns, if necessary.

The predominant use case of a GridPane is form input. Thus, an example might look like

```
val gp = GridPane().apply{ style="""
  -fx-border-width: 1em;
  -fx-border-color: #0000;
  -fx-hgap: 0.5em;
  -fx-vgap: 0.5em;
""" } // just some styling, to make it look more appealing

with(gp) {
    add( Text("Name (last, first):"),
       0,0)  // column, row
    add( HBox(
           TextField().apply{id="lastName"},
           TextField().apply{id="firstName"}
        ),
       1,0, 2,1) // column, row, colspan, rowspan
    add( Text("Street:"),
       0,1)
    add( HBox(
           TextField().apply{id="bldg";prefColumnCount=6},
           TextField().apply{id="street"}
        ),
       1,1, 2,1)
    add( Text("City:"),
       0,2)
    add( HBox(
           TextField().apply{id="city";prefColumnCount=15},
```

```
            TextField().apply{id="state";prefColumnCount=2}
        ),
    1,2, 2,1)
add( Text("Zip:"),
    0,3)
add( TextField().apply{id="zip";prefColumnCount=8},
    1,3, 2,1)
add( Button("SUBMIT").apply{
    setOnAction{
        println(listOf("lastName","firstName","bldg",
                        "street","city","state","zip")
            .map{ k ->
                (scene1.lookup("#${k}") as TextField).text
            })
    }
    },
    0,4)
}
```

```
... add gp to scene ...
```

So you use

```
val gp = GridPane()
gp.add(someNode, column, row)
```

to place some node at a certain cell (indexes zero based) and

```
val gp = GridPane()
gp.add(someNode, column, row, colSpan, rowSpan)
```

to also prescribe a column and row span.

The outcome of this example is shown in Figure 4-4.

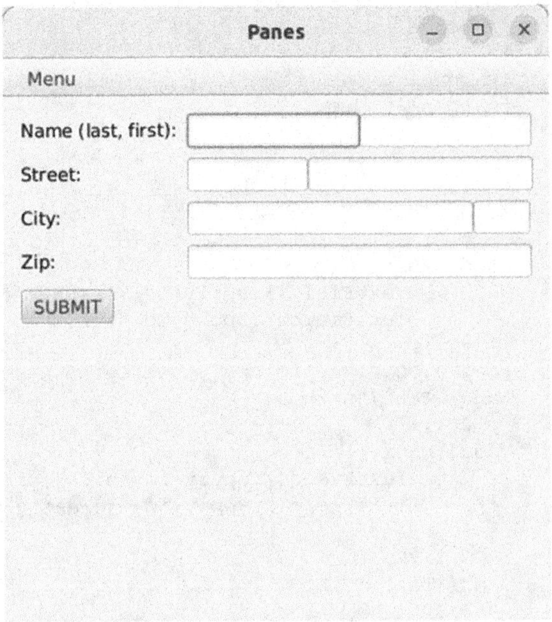

Figure 4-4 A GridPane

By default, rows and columns will be sized to fit their content, and children will be resized according to the widest child in each column (taking the preferred width) and the highest child in each row (taking the preferred height).

In order to add some global spacing between the cells, or to add some margin to some particular cell, write

```
val gp = GridPane().apply{ hgap = 5.0; vgap = 3.0 }

val node:Node = ...
GridPane.setMargin(node, Insets(20.0,10.0,20.0,10.0))
// now add node to the GridPane...
```

Note In the example, we used CSS for setting gaps between the cells.

There is only a no-args constructor for `GridPane`. It would be nice if there was another constructor for specifying the horizontal and vertical gaps between the cells. This is a good place to show Kotlin's strength again. Do you remember the `util.kt` extension collection we introduced in Chapter 1? We use that file again and add two pseudo-constructors to `GridPane`:

```
fun GridPane(hgap:Double, vgap:Double): GridPane =
    GridPane().apply {
        this.hgap = hgap
        this.vgap = vgap
    }

fun GridPane(hgap:Int, vgap:Int): GridPane =
    GridPane(hgap.toDouble(), vgap.toDouble())
```

We provided two variants, one for integer and one for double valued parameters. In order to use it, you can now write

```
import book.kotlinfx.util.*
...
val gp = GridPane(6, 4)
```

TilePane

A TilePane lays out its children in tiles of uniform size. The width and height of each tile are the maximum preferred width and height of all children.

For a horizontal TilePane (the default), the tiles get arranged left-to-right, wrapping at the right border. For a vertical TilePane, the tiles get arranged top-to-bottom, wrapping at the bottom border. You specify the orientation in the constructor:

```
val htp = TilePane(Orientation.HORIZONTAL)
// Or, since horizontal is the default:
//      = TilePane()

val vtp = TilePane(Orientation.VERTICAL)
```

Figure 4-5 A TilePane

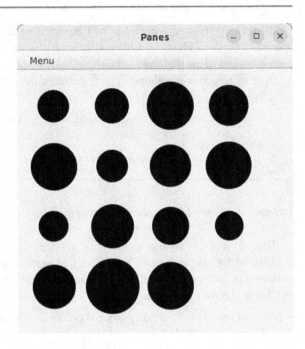

Although, depending on the parent container's layouting, the preferred size of the TilePane might not play a role, you should specify the number of tiles before wrapping:

```
val htp = TilePane()
    .apply{ prefColumns = 7 }

// or

val vtp = TilePane(Orientation.VERTICAL)
    .apply{ prefRows = 7 }
```

An example for using TilePanes reads (for the outcome, see Figure 4-5)

```
val root = TilePane().apply{ style="""
  -fx-border-width: 1em;
  -fx-border-color: #0000;
  -fx-hgap: 0.5em;
  -fx-vgap: 0.5em;
""" }

(1..15).forEach {
    root.children.add(
        Circle(20.0 + 20.0 * Math.random())
    )
}

// add root to scene
```

In order to add some global spacing between the tiles, or to add some margin to some particular tile, write

```
val tp = TilePane().apply{ hgap = 5.0; vgap = 3.0 }

val node:Node = ...
TilePane.setMargin(node, Insets(20.0,10.0,20.0,10.0))
// now add node to the TilePane...
```

Figure 4-6 A BorderPane

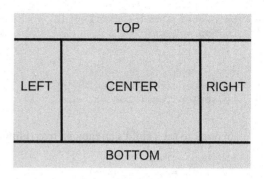

BorderPane

A BorderPane lays out five children at positions:

- **TOP**
  On top. Gets stretched to: Width of the pane, preferred height. If the child cannot be resized to fit within its position, it gets aligned at Pos.TOP_LEFT.
- **BOTTOM**
  On bottom. Gets stretched to: Width of the pane, preferred height. If the child cannot be resized to fit within its position, it gets aligned at Pos.BOTTOM_LEFT.
- **LEFT**
  At left. Gets stretched to: Preferred width, height from TOP to BOTTOM, not overlapping. If the child cannot be resized to fit within its position, it gets aligned at Pos.TOP_LEFT.
- **RIGHT**
  At right. Gets stretched to: Preferred width, height from TOP to BOTTOM, not overlapping. If the child cannot be resized to fit within its position, it gets aligned at Pos.TOP_RIGHT.
- **CENTER**
  At the center. Gets stretched to: All that is left. If the child cannot be resized to fit within its position, it gets aligned at Pos.CENTER.

See Figure 4-6.

The `BorderPane` class has an empty constructor, but also a constructor for directly specifying all children, or just the center. In any case, you can set the children via five predefined methods.

```
val bp = BorderPane()

//val bp = BorderPane(center:Node, top:Node, right:Node,
//    bottom:Node, left:Node)

//val bp = BorderPane(center:Node)

with(bp){
  center = Text("CENTER")
  top = Text("TOP")
  right = Text("RIGHT")
  bottom = Text("BOTTOM")
  left = Text("LEFT")
}

// or, what is the same:
```

```
bp.center = Text("CENTER")
bp.top = Text("TOP")
// ...

// or, what is the same:
bp.setCenter(Text("CENTER"))
bp.setTop(Text("TOP"))
// ...
```

In order to set a child's alignment, overriding the defaults, or to add a margin to a child, you write

```
val top = Text("TOP")
val root = BorderPane()

BorderPane.setAlignment(top, Pos.TOP_CENTER)
BorderPane.setMargin(top, Insets(10.0,0.0,10.0,0.0))

bp.top = top
```

AnchorPane

An AnchorPane lays out its children using constraints specifying offsets from child borders to pane borders. It uses its children's preferred sizes, unless a child is anchored on opposite sides of the pane, in which case the child gets stretched. If this is not possible, only the top/left anchors get honored.

You use one of the companion methods `AnchorPane.setXxxAnchor(` `n:Node,` `dist:Double)` (with Xxx being one of "Left," "Right," "Bottom," "Top") to set anchor distances and an empty constructor or a constructor with node varargs to instantiate the AnchorPane:

```
val txt1 = Text("RIGHT-TOP")
val txt2 = Text("LEFT-BOTTOM")
AnchorPane.setTopAnchor(txt1, 30.0)
AnchorPane.setRightAnchor(txt1, 50.0)
AnchorPane.setBottomAnchor(txt2, 30.0)
AnchorPane.setLeftAnchor(txt2, 50.0)

val root = AnchorPane()
root.children.addAll(txt1, txt2, ...)

// or:
//    val root = AnchorPane(txt1, txt2, ...)

... add root to scene...
```

In order to remove a particular constraint, or to remove all constraints from some child, you can write

```
AnchorPane.setTopAnchor(txt1, null)

// Remove all:
AnchorPane.clearConstraints(txt1)
```

Styling Panes

JavaFX considerably differs from the former Swing UI technology by allowing for a CSS-like styling of layouts and graphical UI elements. I say "CSS-like" because, although many concepts and constructs of the official CSS specification (version 2.1) also apply for JavaFX, not all that CSS has to offer can also be used for our purposes.

In this section, we talk about the JavaFX way of using CSS for styling panes. We don't give a thorough introduction into CSS, and we cannot talk about each and every detail – the topic is just too big, and I don't want to bloat the book too much. Also, the styling of visual elements in contrast to containers is left to a later chapter.

If you want to dive deeper into that matter, and for more details, please visit https://openjfx.io/javadoc/19/javafx.graphics/javafx/scene/doc-files/cssref.html.

Note It is also possible to add individual styles to panes (and nodes in general) via `setStyle()` or `pane.style = ...`. We don't talk about this technique in the book, since using stylesheet documents is the more genuine way of applying CSS.

Adding Stylesheets to the Whole Scene

We already added stylesheets to scenes. Simply create a stylesheet file of any name you like inside folder `src/main/resources/css`, and inside your code write

```
val scene = Scene(...).apply {
    stylesheets.add("css/styleSheetName.css")
}
```

You actually don't have to use that `css/` folder for stylesheet files, but it helps structuring your application.

Adding Stylesheets to Individual Panes

The `Parent` class, which every pane inherits from, has a `getStylesheets()` method you can use to register stylesheets on a per-pane basis:

```
val vb = VBox(...).apply {
    stylesheets.add("css/styles.css")
}
// ... or any other pane

// Or, which is the same
val vb = VBox(...)
vb.stylesheets.add("css/styles.css")
```

The styles specified in the stylesheet can manipulate the node it is assigned to and any nodes down the hierarchy (children and their children aso.).

The CSS selectors to be used for such pane-relative stylesheets are *not* relative themselves. This normally doesn't impose any problem, because of the flexible resolution rules for CSS selectors. It means however that, for example, in a hierarchy like

```
VBox - id="container" {
    HBox - class="name" {
```

```
            Text
        }
    }
```

with a stylesheet assigned to the HBox, for clarity reasons, you may use a CSS selector like shown
here:

```
#container .name Text { -fx-font-size:30px; }
```

and it still points to the Text control, even though `#container` somewhat lies out of the scope of
the stylesheet. However, you cannot use a stylesheet to manipulate nodes up the hierarchy – so a CSS
selector

```
#container
```

specified in the HBox's stylesheet does not change the styles of the parent of the HBox node.

JavaFX CSS Selectors for Panes

A stylesheet file contains a number of rules:

```
selector-chain {
    property:value;
    property:value;
    ...
}
```

The selector-chain designates nodes which then get styles assigned to via "property: value;; pairs. It
consists of a space-separated list of selectors:

- **The Universal Selector "*"**
  Matches any element in the node hierarchy.
- **Type Selectors**
  Use the *simple class name* like `StackPane`, `VBox`, `Text`, `TextField`, ... to select elements by
  type. Every `Node` has a `getTypeSelector()` method (or `.typeSelector` in Kotlin) that
  returns this type name.
- **Class Selectors**
  Use `.clazz` to select elements by class "clazz." Inside the application, you assign one or more
  classes to nodes via

  ```
  Node().apply{styleClass.add("class")}
  - or -
  Node().apply{
     styleClass.addAll("class1", "class2", ...)
  }
  ```

  where `Node()` creates any node (including containers), like in `VBox ( ... )` or `Text ( "Text"`
  `)`.
- **ID Selectors**
  For selecting by a unique ID in CSS, you write `#someID`, and for assigning IDs, use

  ```
  Node().apply{id = "someID"}
  ```

Table 4.1 Pseudo-Classes
for Panes

PSEUDO-CLASS	DESCRIPTION
:disabled	The pane is disabled. Applies when the `disabled` property is true.
:focused	The pane has the focus. Applies when the `focused` property is true.
:hover	The mouse hovers over the pane. Applies when the `hover` property is true.
:pressed	The primary mouse button is pressed on the pane. Applies when the `pressed` property is true.

A child selector ">" like in

```
#container > Text { -fx-font-size:30px; }
```

makes sure only immediate children get selected, no grandchildren and none of their children aso. Adjacent siblings via "+" and structural pseudo-classes are not supported.

Nonstructural pseudo-classes may be used to add a considerable amount of dynamics to frontends. You specify pseudo-classes as follows:

```
selector:pseudo-class { property:value; ... }

- example: change the fill color if the mouse
- is over a node
#nodeId:hover { -fx-fill: blue; }
```

You can of course add pseudo-classes also to individual selectors inside a selector chain.

The most important container pane–related pseudo-classes that are supported are shown in Table 4.1.

JavaFX CSS Properties for Panes

A nonexhaustive collection of pane-related properties is shown in Table 4.2.

For the other properties and more details, see https://openjfx.io/javadoc/19/javafx.graphics/javafx/scene/doc-files/cssref.html.

There is no "margin" property in JavaFX you could use to add an invisible margin around nodes (including containers). There however is a workaround for containers (it doesn't work very well for visual elements). Write and use

```
.pseudo-margin {
  -fx-padding: 1em;
  -fx-border-insets: 1em;
  -fx-background-insets: 1em;
}
```

(or any suitable other CSS selector) in order to achieve almost the same effect.

Table 4.2 Pane CSS Properties

PROPERTY	DESCRIPTION
-fx-padding	One padding value or a set of four padding values (for the top, right, bottom, and left edges), separated by spaces. A value is a number, followed by one of px	mm	cm	in	pt	pc	em	ex (pixel, millimeter, centimeter, inches, points, picas = 12pt, font-size, "x"-height). If only one value is given, it applies to all four edges. A padding is the extra space between the edges and the interior of a pane.
-fx-min-height -fx-pref-height -fx-max-height	A value for the min, pref, or max height of the pane. Possible values are the same as before for the -fx-padding property.
-fx-min-width-fx-pref-width-fx-max-width	A value for the min, pref, or max width of the pane. Possible values are the same as before for the -fx-padding property.
-fx-background-color	Specifies a background color. Values are one of the following: a named color like "green," "blue," etc. (there are many of those; see https://openjfx.io/javadoc/19/javafx.graphics/javafx/scene/doc-files/cssref.html#typecolor); an RGB color like #A73, #FF8034, `rgb( 255, 128, 40 )`, or `rgb( 100%, 50%, 25% )`; or an RGBA color (the fourth component is the Alpha value specifying the opacity, 0.0..1.0) like `rgba( 255, 128, 64, 0.3 )` or `rgba( 100%, 50%, 25%, 0.3 )`. It is also possible to specify gradients for this property – the docs give more information about that.
| -fx-background-image | A background image to use. The value must be a URI, but in the majority of cases, you will refer to an image from the resources, like in<br><br>```
#someId {
  -fx-background-image:
      url(../images/background.png);
png);
}
```<br><br>where the CSS file is placed in `src/main/resources/css` and the image file in `src/main/resources/images`. |
-fx-background-size	If a background image is used, this property specifies its sizing. The value can be SIZE or SIZE SIZE, where the former is for both width and height, and the latter is for width and height, respectively. SIZE can be as described earlier for the -fx-padding property or the string `auto` (tries to preserve the image's natural aspect ratio). As a property value, you can also use one of `cover` (preserves aspect ratio, the whole background gets filled, leading to clipping), `contain` (preserves aspect ratio, the whole image gets shown, leading to blank areas), or `stretch`.
-fx-background-repeat	Whether and how to repeat background images to prevent for otherwise blank areas. Value: one of `repeat-x`, `repeat-y`, or `repeat` (for both). For other options, see the documentation.
-fx-background-position	Where to position a background image. The value can be one of `top`, `right`, `bottom`, `left`, `center`. Or combined `top right`, `top left`, `bottom right`, `bottom left`. Or with offsets added `top 1em right 100px`, ... Offsets can also be specified as percentages: `top 20% right 100px`, ...

(continued)
```

Table 4.2 (continued)

PROPERTY	DESCRIPTION
-fx-background-insets	Any insets between the background and the border. One value refers to all four top, right, bottom, and left edges. Four space-separated values refer to the top, right, bottom, and left edges, respectively. Each distance is a number plus a unit, as described earlier for the -fx-padding property.
-fx-border-width	Use this to set a border width. One value for all borders or four space-separated values for the top, right, bottom, and left borders. Each width value is a number plus a unit, as described earlier for the -fx-padding property.
-fx-border-color	One color value for all borders or four space-separated values for the top, right, bottom, and left borders. Each color value gets specified as described earlier for the -fx-background-color property. For borders painted from image pixels, see the documentation.
-fx-border-style	Used to specify the border stroke style. The value is one of none, solid, dotted, or dashed. For other options, see the documentation.
-fx-alignment	Only for FlowPane, GridPane, HBox, VBox, StackPane, and TilePane. Specifies the alignment of children that cannot be resized to the full extent of the pane or their reserved area. The value is one of top-left, top-center, top-right, center-left, center, center-right, bottom-left, bottom-center, bottom-right, baseline-left, baseline-center, or baseline-right.
-fx-hgap-fx-vgap	Only for FlowPane, GridPane, HBox, and VBox. Horizontal and vertical gaps between children. The value is a number plus a unit, as described earlier for the -fx-padding property.
-fx-column-halignment	Only for FlowPane. The horizontal alignment of children in columns. One of left (default), center, or right.
-fx-row-valignment	Only for FlowPane. The vertical alignment of children in rows. One of top, center (default), baseline, or bottom.
-fx-orientation	Only for FlowPane and TilePane. The primary orientation of children. One of horizontal (default) or vertical.
-fx-grid-lines-visible	Only for GridPane. Whether or not grid lines are visible. One of false (default) or true.
-fx-spacing	Only for HBox and VBox. Set the spacing between children. The value is a number plus a unit, as described earlier for the -fx-padding property.
-fx-fill-height	Only for HBox. Whether or not the pane tries to stretch the heights of its children beyond their preferred height to match the height of the row (if needed). One of false or true (default).
-fx-fill-width	Only for VBox. Whether or not the pane tries to stretch the widths of its children beyond their preferred widths to match the width of the row (if needed). One of false or true (default).
-fx-pref-rows-fx-pref-columns	Only for TilePane. The number of preferred rows and columns. The value is an integer; the default is 5.
-fx-pref-tile-width-fx-pref-tile-height	Only for TilePane. Normally, tiles get sized after the largest of its children. If you instead want to prescribe a preferred size, use these properties. Each value is a number plus a unit, as described earlier for the -fx-padding property.
-fx-tile-alignment	Only for TilePane. Controls the alignment of the children inside their tile area. Possible values are the same as for the property -fx-alignment described earlier.

Summary

In this chapter, we learned about containers (or panes), how to define and configure them, and how to add children to them. For styling purposes, we can use CSS, as known from web technologies. We can assign CSS IDs and classes to containers:

```
SomeContainerClass().apply{
    id = "someID"
    styleClass.add("clazz")
}
```

allowing for various styling properties that can be defined in CSS files like

```
#someID {
    -fx-background-color: red;
    -fx-spacing: 1.5em;
    ...
}

.clazz {
    -fx-padding: 3mm;
    ...
}
```

In a Gradle build environment, you add such CSS files, for example, "styles.css", to folder

```
src/main/resources/css
```

and you assign them to panes via

```
val cont = SomeContainerClass().apply{
    stylesheets.add("css/styles.css")
}
```

Visual Nodes

5

We use the notion *visual node* to draw a distinction between container nodes, which are used to group and lay out a couple of child nodes, and such nodes that have some kind of visual appearance, apart from borders and backgrounds, and including nodes the user can interact with.

In this chapter, we also talk about nodes that contain children, but besides their ability to serve as a parent also provide interactivity. This group comprises ScrollPanes, Accordions, TabPanes, and SplitPanes.

Node Coordinate Systems

A node's position and size get described by different coordinate systems: the coordinate system controlled by the screen, another one controlled by the stage, one more controlled by the scene, and those controlled by the node's parent and the node itself. You usually don't have to think about them often, since JavaFX performs position and size calculations under the hood, given the scene graph and your container selection, more precisely said the type of containers you choose to place your nodes in and what container-related properties you specify.

Once in a while however, it *is* important to take a closer look at positioning and sizing matters. This is where a node's different kinds of boundaries come into play, in detail:

- **layoutBounds**
  Solely based on the geometric properties of a node, disregarding effects, clipping, and transformations.
- **boundsInLocal**
  Based on the geometric properties of a node, including effects and clipping, but disregarding transformations.
- **boundsInParent**
  Based on the geometric properties of a node, including effects, clipping, and transformations. The coordinate space used is the one from the parent.

P. Späth, *Frontend Development with JavaFX and Kotlin*,
https://doi.org/10.1007/978-1-4842-9717-9_5

Figure 5-1 VBox with
Modified Children

Consider the following example:

```
val vb = VBox(
  Button("Button"),
  Button("Button with Effect").apply{
    effect = DropShadow()
  },
  Button("Button with Rotation").apply{
    effect = DropShadow()
    rotate = 30.0
  }
)
... add vb to Scene ...
```

The outcome is shown in Figure 5-1.

Our expectation would have been that a VBox laid out its children in a nonoverlapping manner. So what happened here? As a matter of fact, a VBox (or HBox) calculates its children's effective bounds based on their layoutBounds property, thus not taking effects and transformations into account. If you want to change that, there is an easy technique you can apply: just wrap each child in question into a Group (package javafx.scene, module javafx.graphics):

```
val vb = VBox(
  Group(
    Button("Button")
  ),
  Group(
    Button("Button with Effect").apply{
      effect = DropShadow()
  } ),
  Group(
    Button("Button with Rotation").apply{
      effect = DropShadow()
      rotate = 30.0
  } )
)
... add vb to Scene ...
```

A Group respects the boundsInParent property of its children and presents it to its own parent as layoutBounds. This time, the VBox parent lays out its children without overlapping regions; see Figure 5-2.

Figure 5-2 VBox with
Children in Groups

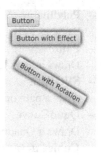

For each bound type, there is a getter you can use in your code:

```
val bnds1:Bounds = someNode.layoutBounds
val bnds2:Bounds = someNode.boundsInLocal
val bnds3:Bounds = someNode.boundsInParent

// --- or, use the properties:

val pr1:ReadOnlyObjectProperty<Bounds> =
    someNode.layoutBoundsProperty()
val pr2:ReadOnlyObjectProperty<Bounds> =
    someNode.boundsInLocalProperty()
val pr3:ReadOnlyObjectProperty<Bounds> =
    someNode.boundsInParentProperty()
```

There are no setters, though, since the values are computed. Correspondingly, the properties are read-only properties.

Shapes

Shapes are nodes that show something, but provide no means for the user to provide input. Prominent examples are texts without editing capabilities and geometric figures like lines, curves, rectangles, circles, and ellipses. The full list of built-in shapes reads

- **Text**
  Writes some text on a scene. One line or several lines are possible. Use \n as a line separator; in addition, texts get automatically wrapped if you specify a `wrappingWidth`.
- **Rectangle**
  Draws a rectangle.
- **Circle**
  Draws a circle.
- **Line**
  Draws a line.
- **Ellipse**
  Draws an ellipse.
- **Arc**
  Draws an arc of a circle or of an ellipse.
- **Polygon**
  Draws an automatically closed polygon.

– **Polyline**
Same as Polygon, but does not automatically close the perimeter.
– **Path**
Draws a path. Elements like lines and curves get added programmatically.
– **SVGPath**
Adds a path defined by an SVG string.
– **QuadCurve**
Draws a Quadratic Bézier Curve.
– **CubicCurve**
Draws a Cubic Bézier Curve.

To add a shape to a scene does not differ from what you do with any other type of node, as the following example shows:

```
val path = Path().apply {
    strokeWidth = 3.0
    with(elements){
      add(MoveTo(0.0,0.0))
      add(LineTo(50.0,20.0))
      add(LineTo(20.0,50.0))
} }

val circle = Circle(30.0)

val text1 = Text("""Some text
    |Second line""".trimMargin())

val text2 = Text("Some long text ".repeat(10))
    .apply{ wrappingWidth = 300.0 }

val vb = VBox(
  path,
  circle,
  text1,
  text2
)
... add vb to scene ...
```

We already used text nodes quite often in the book, and there is of course more to say about this kind of node. First of all, we can apply a couple of styles to texts, like font, size, and colors. This is best achieved via CSS, and we will talk about it later in this chapter. The following list shows a few more interesting properties texts can have besides those controlled via CSS:

– **Line breaks**
Add an \n anywhere in the text string to force line breaks.
– **wrappingWidth**
This is a property of the Text class. If you set it via, for example:

```
            val txt = Text("Dear Mrs. Smith, ...")
              .apply{wrappingWidth=250.0}
```

you can prescribe a text width limit where automatic wrapping will happen. Since there is an accordingly named property getter, text.wrappingWidthProperty(), you can bind this property to other properties, for example, the container's width.

- **lineSpacing**

  This is another `Text` property. You can use it to add some extra spacing between the lines in a multiline text. Write

  ```
  val txt = Text("Dear Mrs. Smith, ...")
      .apply{lineSpacing=5.0}
  ```

  in order to use it.

- **nodeOrientation**

  A property inherited from the `Node` class. Normally, the text flow is left-to-right, but you can change it via

  ```
  val txt = Text("... عِلمًا زِدْنِي رَبِّ")
      .apply{nodeOrientation =
              NodeOrientation.RIGHT_TO_LEFT}
  ```

  For more details about `Text` nodes and all the other shape classes, see the API documentation at https://openjfx.io/javadoc/19/javafx.graphics/javafx/scene/shape/Shape.html.

Canvas

A Canvas allows us to access the graphics system using low-level operations. There is no node hierarchy, and hence there are no containers – you have to calculate all coordinates yourself.

It is easy to add canvases to a scene. Consider the following code that paints random rectangles:

```
import javafx.scene.text.*
import book.kotlinfx.util.*
import javafx.scene.canvas.Canvas
...

val canvas = Canvas(450.0, 300.0)

val vb = VBox(
    Button("Paint Rectangle"){
        val w = 20.0 + 400.0 * Math.random()
        val h = 20.0 + 180.0 * Math.random()
        val x = (450.0 - w) * Math.random()
        val y = (300.0 - h) * Math.random()
        val red = Math.random()
        val green = Math.random()
        val blue = Math.random()
        val opacity = 0.2 + 0.8 * Math.random()
        val g = canvas.graphicsContext2D
        g.fill = Color(red,green,blue,opacity)
        g.fillRect(x,y,w,h)
    },
    canvas
)
... add vb to the scene ...
```

The outcome is shown in Figure 5-3.

There are many kinds of objects you can paint on canvases. The API documentation at https://openjfx.io/javadoc/19/javafx.graphics/javafx/scene/canvas/Canvas.html tells you more.

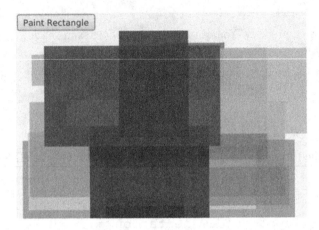

Figure 5-3 Rectangles Drawn in a Canvas

Image Nodes

In order to place images somewhere on your scene graph, use the `ImageView` class, a subclass of `Node`:

```
val img = ImageView(Image("images/frog.jpg"))
... add img to scene ...
```

In a Gradle build setup, the image files go to `src/main/resources` (*including* any subfolder, so for the preceding example code, you'd use folder `src/main/resources/images`).

Controls

Nodes of type *control* allow the user to enter some text, click something, shift something, select something, switch something, or in general somehow react on the user performing GUI actions. In the following paragraphs, we take a survey of such control nodes.

Text Fields and Text Areas

TextField and TextArea allow the user to add a single-line or multiline text, respectively. A no-args constructor creates an empty TextField or TextArea; see Figure 5-4.

```
import javafx.scene.text.*
import book.kotlinfx.util.*
import javafx.scene.canvas.Canvas
...

val tf1 = TextField()
val ta1 = TextArea()

val vb = VBox(
  tf1,
  tf2
)
... add vb to the scene ...
```

Figure 5-4 Simple
TextField and TextArea

Note JavaFX does us a favor and automatically sets the input focus on the first control of a scene.

In order to set an initial node value, you write

```
val tf2 = TextField("Hello World")
val ta2 = TextArea("Hello World\nLine 2")
```

We learn later how to set styles, including the size, via CSS. But it is also possible to set the row size (for TextField) or both the row and column sizes (for TextArea) programmatically:

```
val tf4 = TextField().apply{
  prefColumnCount = 24
  maxWidth = Region.USE_PREF_SIZE  }
val ta4 = TextArea().apply{
  prefColumnCount = 24
  prefRowCount = 3
  maxWidth = Region.USE_PREF_SIZE
  maxHeight = Region.USE_PREF_SIZE  }
```

The maxWidth = ... and maxHeight = ... statements are needed to prevent for the container to stretch the controls beyond their preferred dimension. Depending on which container you use, you might omit these statements.

You can avoid adding labels to text fields or text areas by setting a prompt text:

```
val tf5 = TextField().apply{
  promptText = "Enter something" }
val ta5 = TextArea().apply{
  promptText = "Enter something" }
```

The prompt does not contribute to the node's value and disappears once you enter something.

To get or set the text, you can use the .text accessor: textField.text = ... or ... = textField.text (same for TextArea). However, you almost never should do that. A much more elegant and architecturally more stable way to connect text input controls to model values is to use *binding*. The following listing shows an example:

```
class PersonModel {
  val firstName = SimpleStringProperty()
  val lastName = SimpleStringProperty()
}

val pm = PersonModel()

val gp = GridPane(5.0,5.0).apply{
    add(Text("First Name:"),
        0,0)
    add(TextField().apply{ textProperty().
```

```
                   bindBidirectional(pm.firstName) },
              1,0)
           add(Text("Last Name:"),
              0,1)
           add(TextField().apply{ textProperty().
                   bindBidirectional(pm.lastName) },
              1,1)
        }

    ... add gp to scene ...
```

Can you see the advantage? No need to add change listeners to the controller nodes, no need to add data transfer buttons, and the model classes don't have to know anything about the GUI classes! Likewise, we can put any persistence, validation, and data transformation code into the model classes, away from the GUI. But we can even do better – adding a property binding is such a common task that we can add a pseudo-constructor to util.kt (package book.kotlinfx.util):

```
fun TextField(sp:StringProperty) = TextField().apply {
    textProperty().bindBidirectional(sp) }
fun TextArea(sp:StringProperty) = TextArea().apply {
    textProperty().bindBidirectional(sp) }
```

In the GUI code, we can now write

```
import book.kotlinfx.util.*
...

class PersonModel {
  val firstName = SimpleStringProperty()
  val lastName = SimpleStringProperty()
}

val pm = PersonModel()

val gp = GridPane(5.0,5.0).apply{
      add(Text("First Name:"),      0,0)
      add(TextField(pm.firstName), 1,0)
      add(Text("Last Name:"),       0,1)
      add(TextField(pm.lastName),  1,1)
    }

    ... add gp to scene ...
```

Of course, model classes should go to their own package. Just for demonstration purposes, we put them into JavaFX's frontend controller class.

Action Buttons

Buttons with some press action listener get implemented as

```
import javafx.scene.control.*
...

val btn1 = Button("Klick me").apply {
  setOnAction{ event ->
    println("Button pressed")
  }
}

    ... add btn1 to scene ...
```

If you don't need the event instance inside the action handler, you can just write

```
val btn1 = Button("Klick me").apply {
  setOnAction{ _ ->
    println("Button pressed")
  }
}
```

And since defining a button label plus an action handler is such a common pattern, we can provide a pseudo-constructor inside util.kt (package book.kotlinfx.util):

```
fun Button(label: String, action: Button.() -> Unit)
    : Button =
  Button(label).apply {
    setOnAction { _ -> action() }
  }
```

Now it is possible to write

```
import book.kotlinfx.util.*
...

val btn1 = Button("Klick me") {
    println("Button pressed")
    // println("I am " + this.toString())
}
```

Note In case you don't understand the Button.() -> ... construct in the pseudo-constructor earlier, it is called *function type with receiver*, and it makes sure the function block gets executed in the context of the Button class. You can directly access the button by using this.

Buttons can be styled via CSS – we'll talk about that later in the chapter.

Button Bars

Especially for YES, NO, and CANCEL buttons in dialogs, the button order becomes interesting, since the operating system has its own idea how to lay out such buttons. Fortunately, JavaFX helps us to correctly position such buttons. Consider the following example:

```
import book.kotlinfx.util.*
...

  lateinit var stage:Stage
  ...

  val bb = ButtonBar().apply{ buttons.addAll(
    Button("Yes"){ println("YES pressed") }.apply{
      ButtonBar.setButtonData(this,
                              ButtonData.YES) },
    Button("No"){ println("NO pressed") }.apply{
      ButtonBar.setButtonData(this,
                              ButtonData.NO) },
    Button("Close"){ stage.close() }.apply{
      ButtonBar.setButtonData(this,
                              ButtonData.CANCEL_CLOSE) }
  ) }
```

```
stage = Stage().apply{
    // add scene to stage...
    // add bb to scene...
}
```

A ButtonBar essentially is an HBox, and via its static method `.setButtonData()`, it ensures a correct ordering of its child button nodes.

Menus

In order to add a menu to your application, you basically use a combination of `MenuBar`, `Menu`, and `MenuItem` classes:

```
val txt = Text() // for demonstration

val mb = MenuBar(
  Menu("File", null,
    MenuItem("Open"){ txt.text = "Open clicked" },
    MenuItem("Save"){ txt.text = "Save clicked" },
    SeparatorMenuItem(),
    MenuItem("Quit"){ txt.text = "Quit clicked" }
  ),
  Menu("Edit", null,
    MenuItem("Find"){ txt.text = "Find clicked" },
    MenuItem("Replace"){
        txt.text = "Replace clicked" },
    Menu("Statistics",null,
        MenuItem("Words"){
            txt.text = "Words clicked" },
        MenuItem("Characters"){
            txt.text = "Characters clicked" }
    )
  )
)

val vb = VBox(
    mb,
    VBox(txt).apply{ padding = Insets(10.0) }
)

... add vb to scene ...
```

You can use a node as a second argument in the `Menu()` constructor for adding a menu icon as in

```
Menu("Menu",
    ImageView(Image("images/img.png")),
    item1, ...)
```

Or, if you want to scale the image to a certain size:

```
Menu("Menu",
    ImageView(Image("images/img.png",
                    20.0,20.0,false,true)),
    item1, ...)
```

Place the image files in folder `src/main/resources/images` for this to work.

For context menus, the approach is very similar. Instead of `MenuBar`, you use `ContextMenu`, and you assign the context menu to any control node via `.contextMenu = ...`:

```
val editWithContextMenu = TextField().apply {
  text = "Click Mouse-Right for context menu"
  contextMenu = ContextMenu(
      MenuItem("Clear"){ this.text = "" },
      MenuItem("Hello"){ this.text = "Hello" }
  )
}
```

Toolbars

A toolbar often appears right underneath the main menu of an application. The ToolBar class acts like an HBox or VBox, but automatically adds an overflow button if not all child buttons fit into the space provided by the parent container:

```
val tb = ToolBar()
(1..20).forEach{ i ->
  tb.items.add( Button("Button #${i}") )
}

val vb = VBox(
    tb
)
... add vb to scene ...
```

Checkboxes

Adding checkboxes in JavaFX is easy. We already talked about the importance of separating model and view code, so the following example shows the proper way of using checkboxes:

```
import book.kotlinfx.util.*
...

class PersonModel {
  var firstName = SimpleStringProperty()
  var lastName = SimpleStringProperty()
  var employed = SimpleBooleanProperty()
}
val p1 = PersonModel()

val gp = GridPane(5.0,5.0).apply {
    add(Text("First name:"), 0,0)
    add(TextField(p1.firstName), 1,0)
    add(Text("Last name:"), 0,1)
    add(TextField(p1.lastName), 1,1)
    add(Text("Employed:"), 0,2)
    add(CheckBox(p1.employed), 1,2)  // <==
}
... add gp to scene ...
```

Of course, the model class should go to a model package – only for demonstration purposes, you can use the GUI class file for that.

In order for this to work, we have to provide the following pseudo-constructors in `util.kt` (package `book.kotlinfx.util`):

```
...
fun TextField(sp:StringProperty) = TextField().apply {
    textProperty().bindBidirectional(sp) }
fun CheckBox(bp:BooleanProperty) = CheckBox().apply {
    selectedProperty().bindBidirectional(bp) }
...
```

It makes sure the binding of the checkbox to the model property happens.

Radio Buttons

If you need radio buttons, that is, a group of checkboxes with at most one item checked, you must place a couple of `RadioButton` nodes anywhere and any way you like on your scene, and you must register all of them with one instance of `ToggleGroup`. That sounds easy so far. It gets more complicated however if we want to connect the radio buttons' status to a model. While each `RadioButton` has a `selectedProperty` and we *could* connect every radio button to its own boolean property inside a model, what we actually want is a single property in the model pointing to the actually selected radio button, using an `Int` or `String` ID.

In order to achieve such a simple connection between a radio button group and a single property, we first add a couple of utility functions to `util.kt`:

```
fun ToggleGroup.addMyListener(
        listener: (value:String) -> Unit) {
  selectedToggleProperty().addListener{_,_,newVal ->
      listener(newVal.userData as String)
  }
}

fun ToggleGroup(listener: (value:String) -> Unit) =
    ToggleGroup().apply{ addMyListener(listener) }

fun ToggleGroup.selectToggle(id:String) {
  selectToggle( toggles.find { it -> it.userData == id } )
}

fun RadioButton(id:String, label:String,
        toggleGroup:ToggleGroup) = RadioButton(label).apply{
  toggleGroup.toggles.add(this)
  this.userData = id
}
```

The first one allows for adding a listener to a `ToggleGroup`. The listener gets informed about selecting buttons from a group. For this purpose, it uses the toggle buttons' `userData` attribute as a string valued ID. The second one simplifies construction of toggle groups. The third one adds a method to `ToggleGroup`, allowing for selecting a radio button by string ID. The last one helps constructing radio buttons given an ID, a label, and a toggle group.

In the view code, we can now write, for example:

```
import book.kotlinfx.util.*   // for util.kt
...

    class FruitModel {
    var selectedId = SimpleStringProperty("Bananas")
```

```
    }
    val f1 = FruitModel()

    // Just an example: observe model changes
    f1.selectedId.addListener{_,_,v ->
      println("Selected: ${v}")
    }

    // A ToggleGroup with a custom listener:
    // Binding the toggle group to the model
    val tg = ToggleGroup{ value:String ->
      f1.selectedId.value = value
    }

    val vb = VBox(
          RadioButton(id="Bananas","Bananas",tg),
          RadioButton(id="Apples","Apples",tg),
          RadioButton(id="Lemons","Lemons",tg),
          RadioButton(id="Other","Other",tg)
    )
    // ... add vb to scene ...

    // Select toggle by model value
    tg.selectToggle( f1.selectedId.value )
```

This can serve as a template for your own radio buttons.

Combo Boxes

If you need a selection of one element given a list of possible choices, the ComboBox node class is your friend. A combo box is semantically not much different from a group of radio buttons, but it presents a drop-down list of its items and thus does not need that much space on the UI.

The following listing shows a combo box of different fruits and also presents a way to bind a combo box to a model:

```
    val FRUITS = FXCollections.observableList(listOf(
        "Bananas", "Apples", "Lemons", "OTHER"))

    class Model {
      var fruit = SimpleStringProperty()
    }
    val fm = Model()

    val combo = ComboBox(FRUITS).apply{
      valueProperty().bindBidirectional(fm.fruit)
    }

    // ... add combo to scene ...
```

A combo box by default shows up to ten items in the choice list. If the number of items is greater, a scrollbar gets presented. If you want to change that number, write, for example:

```
    val combo = ComboBox(...).apply{
        visibleRowCount = 15
    }
```

Sliders

In order to let the user adjust some continuous value by shifting a knob via mouse click-and-drag, you can use a `Slider` node. Sliders can be very simple, without any decorations, or you can add ticks and tick labels. The following code shows two sliders, one horizontal without decorations and another one vertical and with ticks and labels.

```
import book.kotlinfx.util.*
...

    val sl1 = Slider(0.0,100.0,33.0).apply{
      orientation = Orientation.HORIZONTAL
      // <- this is the default, you can just as well
      //    ommit it
    }
    val sl2 = Slider(0.0,100.0,33.0).apply{
      orientation = Orientation.VERTICAL
      setShowTickMarks(true)
      setShowTickLabels(true)
      setMajorTickUnit(25.0)
      setBlockIncrement(10.0) // key up/down incr.
    }

    val vb = VBox(
        sl1, VSTRUT(5),
        sl2
    )
```

The outcome is shown in Figure 5-5.

Binding a slider to a model property is easy, as the following listing shows:

```
    class Model {
      val prop = SimpleDoubleProperty(0.33)
    }
    val m = Model()

    val sl1 = Slider(0.0,100.0,0.0).apply{
      valueProperty().bindBidirectional(m.prop)
    }
```

Figure 5-5 Sliders

Miscellaneous Controls

The following shows a list of additional controls that don't get further explained in this book. For more information, visit https://openjfx.io/javadoc/19/javafx.controls/javafx/scene/control/package-summary.html.

- **ColorPicker**
  Allows for selecting a color value from a palette or a two-dimensional spectrum.
- **DatePicker**
  A date picker helps for entering date via calendar view.
- **Pagination**
  A control tool for paginating large lists.
- **ProgressIndicator**
  A circular control showing the progress state of some ongoing process.
- **Spinner**
  A text input with values from some ordered list. Usually shows a pair of tiny arrows for stepping through the list via mouse clicks.

Control Panes

Panes that provide visual components with some kind of user interoperability are called *control panes*. The following paragraphs describe the control panes JavaFX has to offer.

Scroll Panes

Adding scroll handles to exceedingly large panes (or nodes in general) is easy. Just surround the pane (or node) in question by `ScrollPane { ... }`:

```
val p = SomeLargePaneOrNode()
// ... fill it

val cont = SomeParentPane() // or scene root
cont.children.add( ScrollPane( p ) )

...add cont to scene...
```

For the majority of cases, this is all you have to do. For special cases, there are some properties for tuning behavior and graphical appearance you can set according to your needs. In the following paragraphs, we describe some of them.

First of all, you might want to adjust the visibility policy of the scroll handles. You can achieve this via

```
val sp = ScrollPane( contentsNode ).apply{
  hbarPolicy = ScrollPane.ScrollBarPolicy.ALWAYS
  vbarPolicy = ScrollPane.ScrollBarPolicy.ALWAYS
}

// Or, use the property, which can also be used for
// binding
val sp = ScrollPane( contentsNode ).apply{
  hbarPolicyProperty().bind( someObservable1 )
```

```
  vbarPolicyProperty().bind( someObservable2 )
  // Two-way binding is also possible
}
```

Here, `hbarPolicy` stands for the horizontal and `vbarPolicy` for the vertical bar. The possible constants from `ScrollPane.ScrollBarPolicy` are

– **AS_NEEDED**
  This is the default. Scrollbar and scroll handle get shown only if the horizontal or vertical dimension of the contents exceeds the size of the scroll pane.
– **ALWAYS**
  The scrollbar always gets shown. The scroll handle gets shown only if the horizontal or vertical dimension of the contents exceeds the size of the scroll pane.
– **NEVER**
  Neither scrollbar nor handle get shown, regardless of the horizontal or vertical dimension of the contents exceeding the size of the scroll pane or not. You use this if you don't want the user to adjust what part of the contents gets shown. Panning still might be possible; see the following text.

If the contained node is resizable, you can configure the scroll pane to resize its contents in case the latter is smaller than the pane:

```
val sp = ScrollPane( contentsNode ).apply{
  isFitToWidth = true
  isFitToHeight = true
}

// Or, take the properties, which can also be used for
// binding
sp.fitToWidthProperty().bind( someObservable )
// ...
```

Every scroll pane maintains two `Double` typed values for describing its scroll positions: `hvalue` and `vvalue`. They by default range from 0.0 (leftmost or topmost) to 1.0 (rightmost or bottommost), and you can freely read and set them:

```
import book.kotlinfx.util.*
...

val sp = ScrollPane( contentsNode ).apply{
    vvalue = 0.25
}
val btn = Button("hvalue<-0.0 vvalue<-0.5"){
    sp.hvalue = 0.0
    sp.vvalue = 0.5
}
... add sp and btn to the scene ...
```

Instead, using the corresponding properties gives us the ability to directly connect scrollbars to external properties via binding or to other nodes. For example, in order to automatically write vertical scroll positions to a text node, you'd write

```
import book.kotlinfx.util.*
...

val vValProp = SimpleDoubleProperty(0.0)
val vValStr:ObservableValue<String> =
    bindingNumberToString(vValProp)
```

```
val sp = ScrollPane(
    VBox().apply{ (1..100).forEach{ i ->
        vb.children.add(Text("I'm Text #${i}"))
    } } ).apply{

    // Bind the scrolling position to the text node
    vvalueProperty().bindBidirectional(vValProp)

}

val txt = Text(vValStr)

val container = VBox( 5.0, txt, sp )
... add container to scene ...
```

In order for this to work, we have to provide a utility function `bindingNumberToString()` as a bridge between String and Number (Int, Double, Float, ...) valued properties. Only then we can bind the scrolling position, which is a number, to the String property constituting the text node. In addition, we need a (pseudo-) constructor for `Text`s with a binding property as parameter. Both the function and the pseudo-constructor go to `util.kt`:

```
...
fun Text(observable:ObservableValue<String>) =
    Text().apply{ textProperty().bind(observable) }

// Allows for binding number (Int, Double, ...)
// properties as String observables
fun bindingNumberToString(nmbr:Property<Number>)
        : ObservableValue<String> =
    Bindings.createObjectBinding(
        { -> nmbr.value.toString() }, nmbr )
...
```

You might have noticed that there is nothing that allows us to directly add scroll position change listeners to a scroll pane. However, this can easily be achieved indirectly by using the properties:

```
// Add a listener for vertical scrollbar position changes
sp.vvalueProperty().addListener{
        observable, oldVal, newVal ->
    when(observable) {
        is DoubleProperty -> println(observable.value)
} }
```

The `when() { }` construct is necessary, because the Kotlin compiler cannot infer the precise type of the lambda function parameter.

Moving a scroll handle is not the only way you can shift the viewport around. If you enable *panning*, you can also click-hold-drag with the click performed on the pane's content area to achieve that. You must explicitly enable this feature:

```
val sp = ScrollPane( contentsNode ).apply{
    isPannable = true
}
```

Accordions

In order to achieve an accordion-like effect, you use the `Accordion` class. It has a constructor that accepts a parameter list of `TitledPane` instances, which in turn represent the accordion sheets. The following listing creates such an accordion:

```
val acc = Accordion(
  TitledPane("Pane 1",VBox(
    Text("I am pane #1")
  )),
  TitledPane("Pane 2",VBox(
    Text("I am pane #2")
  )),
  TitledPane("Pane 3",VBox(
    Text("I am pane #3")
  ))
)
// ... add acc to scene ...
```

We can improve the readability a little bit, if we add the following to our utility collection `util.kt`:

```
fun Accordion(pane1:Pair<String,Node>,
    vararg panes:Pair<String,Node>) = Accordion().apply{
  listOf(pane1,*panes).forEach{ pp ->
    this.panes.add(TitledPane(pp.first,pp.second))
  }
}
```

It takes over the job of constructing TitledPanes, so in the view class, we can write

```
import book.kotlinfx.util.* // for util.kt
...

    val acc = Accordion(
      "Pane 1" to VBox(
        Text("I am pane #1")
      ),
      "Pane 2" to VBox(
        Text("I am pane #2")
      ),
      "Pane 3" to VBox(
        Text("I am pane #3")
      )
    )
    // ... add acc to scene ...
```

If you don't recognize the pattern, a `... to ...` generates such a `Pair<>` used in the new pseudo-constructor in the utilities collection.

Tab Panes

For tabbed panes, we use the same simplification as presented for accordions in the preceding section. Therefore, we add a pseudo-constructor for `TabPane` to `util.kt`:

```
fun TabPane(pane1:Pair<String,Node>,
    vararg panes:Pair<String,Node>) = TabPane().apply{
  listOf(pane1,*panes).forEach{ pp ->
```

```
        this.tabs.add(Tab(pp.first,pp.second))
    }
}
```

In the view code, you can then, for example, write

```
import book.kotlinfx.util.* // for util.kt
...
    val tabs = TabPane(
      "Pane 1" to VBox(
        Text("I am pane #1")
      ),
      "Pane 2" to VBox(
        Text("I am pane #2")
      ),
      "Pane 3" to VBox(
        Text("I am pane #3")
      )
    ).apply{
      // tabClosingPolicy = TabPane.
      //       TabClosingPolicy.UNAVAILABLE
    }

    // ... add tabs to scene ...
```

By default, tabs can be closed by the user, which obviously makes sense only if in the application tabs somehow get created dynamically. The preceding code shows you how to disable that feature.

Split Panes

Split panes present two or more panes next to each other, giving the user the opportunity to shift the divider using the mouse. As an example, consider

```
    val p1 = BorderPane( Text("I'm pane 1") )
    val p2 = BorderPane( Text("I'm pane 2") )

    val sp = SplitPane(p1, p2).apply{
        orientation = Orientation.HORIZONTAL
    }
    // ... add sp to scene ...
```

The divider position can be set programmatically, and you can also bind it to a property. For more details, see the API documentation.

Styling Visual Nodes

In Chapter 4, we already talked about using CSS for styling containers. Because in order to style visual and control nodes you usually add CSS stylesheets to the containers (or panes) surrounding them, I do not repeat the procedure of how to apply CSS to your scene. The addressing of view elements is very similar: you assign CSS IDs and/or classes, and in the stylesheets, you use selectors pointing to nodes in the view hierarchy:

```
    VBox(
      TextField().apply{
          id = "node3484"
```

```
        styleClass.add("foreName")
    }
).apply{ styleClass.add("person") }

// CSS stylesheet file:
.person .foreName {
    -fx-text-fill: blue;
}
```

I do not present further details about CSS methodologies here, because it is not much different for visual and controller nodes, and you can switch back to Chapter 4 for more information. Instead, in this section, I describe the most important CSS properties for such noncontainer nodes.

Note Remember to add a stylesheet to a scene, you write

```
val scene = Scene(...).apply {
    stylesheets.add("css/styleSheetName.css")
}
```

For the full list of properties and all JavaFX CSS details, see https://openjfx.io/javadoc/19/javafx. graphics/javafx/scene/doc-files/cssref.html#typelength.

We start with CSS properties applicable to all nodes. Table 5.1 shows an overview.

If needed, you can use one of the following pseudo-classes for selectors: `:disabled` | `:focused` | `:hover` | `:pressed`.

Shape-related properties are shown in Table 5.2.

For `Text` nodes, you can set the font, the tab size, text alignment, aso. Table 5.3 shows you the properties.

Because a `Text` is also a `Shape`, it inherits Shape's properties. Particularly interesting are `-fx-fill` and `-fx-stroke` to set the Text's color.

Table 5.1 Node CSS Properties

PROPERTY	DESCRIPTION
-fx-blend-mode	Describes the blending mode, if the node gets drawn over an area that already contains pixels. One of `add` | `blue` | `color-burn` | `color-dodge` | `darken` | `difference` | `exclusion` | `green` | `hard-light` | `lighten` | `multiply` | `overlay` | `red` | `screen` | `soft-light` | `src-atop` | `src-in` | `src-out` | `src-over`. Default is null.
-fx-cursor	Which cursor to use. One of `null` | `crosshair` | `default` | `hand` | `move` | `e-resize` | `h-resize` | `ne-resize` | `nw-resize` | `n-resize` | `se-resize` | `sw-resize` | `s-resize` | `w-resize` | `v-resize` | `text` | `wait`. Or a URL, for example, `url(http://example.com/images/xyz.png)`. Default is null.
-fx-opacity	The opacity of the node, from 0.0 ... 1.0
. -fx-rotate	A rotation to apply about the center, clockwise in degrees from 3 o'clock.
-fx-scale-x -fx-scale-y -fx-scale-z	A scaling about the center (1.0 means identity).
-fx-translate-x -fx-translate-y -fx-translate-z	A translation in pixels.
visibility	One of `visible` | `hidden` | `collapse` | `inherit`.

Table 5.2 Shape CSS Properties

PROPERTY	DESCRIPTION
-fx-fill	The fill color. Values are one of the following: a named color like "green," "blue," etc. (there are many of those; see https://openjfx.io/javadoc/19/javafx.graphics/javafx/scene/doc-files/cssref.html#typecolor); an RGB color like #A73, #FF8034, rgb(255, 128, 40), or rgb(100%, 50%, 25%); or an RGBA color (the fourth component is the Alpha value specifying the opacity, 0.0..1.0) like rgba(255, 128, 64, 0.3) or rgba(100%, 50%, 25%, 0.3). It is also possible to specify gradients for this property – the docs give more information about that.
-fx-smooth	Whether or not to smooth the shape. One of true | false. Default is true.
-fx-stroke	The stroke color. Values are the same as before for -fx-fill. For more stroke-related properties, see the JavaFX CSS reference.

Table 5.3 Text CSS Properties

PROPERTY	DESCRIPTION
-fx-font	The font to use. The possibilities are endless, but you'll often use values like "16px serif" (or instead of serif any other font available on your system or one of the generic font families: "serif," "sans-serif," "cursive," "fantasy," "monospace"), "bold 20px serif," "italic 20px serif," or "italic bold 20px serif." Or use a comma-separated list to specify several fonts at once – the first one available will be taken.
-fx-strikethrough -fx-underline	Use true or false as value.
-fx-tab-size	Set the tab size. The default is 8
. -fx-text-alignment	One of left | center | right | justify. Default is left.
-fx-text-origin	One of baseline | top | bottom. Default is baseline.

All nodes of type Control, including control panes (Accordion, TabPane, . . .), inherit from Region, which we implicitly talked about in Chapter 4. The properties are -fx-background-color, -fx-background-image, -fx-background-insets, -fx-background-position, -fx-background-radius, -fx-background-repeat, -fx-background-size, -fx-border-radius, -fx-border-style, -fx-border-image-repeat, -fx-border-image-slice, -fx-padding, -fx-position-shape, -fx-scale-shape, -fx-shape, -fx-snap-to-pixel, -fx-region-background, -fx-region-border, -fx-min-height, -fx-pref-height, -fx-max-height, -fx-min-width, -fx-pref-width, -fx-max-width. For details, see Chapter 4 or https://openjfx.io/javadoc/19/javafx.graphics/javafx/scene/doc-files/cssref.html#region (section "Controls").

Note For controls, if they include texts to be shown and/or entered, the name of the text color property to be used is -fx-text-fill.

Summary

In this chapter, we talked about node coordinate systems, shapes (including texts), canvases, image nodes, controls and control-like panes like menus and toolbars, and the styling of visual noncontainer nodes via CSS stylesheets.

Lists and Tables

6

With lists, tables, and trees being rather elaborate and special controls, we did not handle them in Chapter 5, and a discussion of them was postponed to this chapter. Despite being possibly more complex compared to other control nodes, you add them to containers just like any other node type. In the following sections, we talk about creating such collection views and summarize the options for data housekeeping, appearance, and behavior.

Lists with ListView

A ListView can present a number of items in a list, allowing for items to be selected or actions to be initiated if one or more items get selected. In its simplest form, a ListView shows the result of each item's `toString()` call in its cells, but you can customize that; see the following example.

Consider the following code, which shows a ListView for a list of strings:

```
import book.kotlinfx.util.*
...

val l = FXCollections.observableArrayList(
        "Apple","Peach","Banana")
val listView = ListView(l).apply {
    placeholder = Text("The List is empty")
    selectionModel.selectionMode = SelectionMode.MULTIPLE
}
val btn1 = Button("Change it"){
    l.set(1, "Pineapple")
}
val btn2 = Button("Add an item"){
    listView.items.add(
        System.currentTimeMillis().toString())
}
val info = Text("")
listView.selectionModel.getSelectedItems().addListener{
    list:Observable -> info.text = "Selected: ${list}" }

val vb = VBox(
    listView,
    btn1,
    btn2,
```

© The Author(s), under exclusive license to APress Media, LLC, part of Springer Nature 2023
P. Späth, *Frontend Development with JavaFX and Kotlin*,
https://doi.org/10.1007/978-1-4842-9717-9_6

```
      info
).apply{
   btn1.minWidthProperty().bind(this.widthProperty().
      divide(2.0))
   btn2.minWidthProperty().bind(this.widthProperty().
      divide(2.0))
}
```

```
... add vb to scene ...
```

A few observations about this listing are worth mentioning:

- The list view gets constructed with an observable list. Because of that, any change in the list gets immediately reflected in the view.
- A placeholder gets set on the list view. It is shown only if the list is empty. Placeholders are optional, and you can use any kind of node, not just texts as shown here.
- Via `.selectionModel.selectionMode = ...`, we allow for selecting multiple values (use the CTRL and SHIFT keys for that).
- The action closures used for the two buttons show that we can use the original list, but just as well the list retrieved by `.items`.
- The `.addListener{ ... }` shown here adds an `InvalidationListener`. Kotlin automatically infers that.
- The snippet inside `VBox().apply{ ... }` just stretches the two buttons to the same width.

Figure 6-1 shows the application running this code.

In order to tailor the rendering of the ListView cells, we have to assign a `Callback` (package `javafx.util`) to its `cellFactory` property. Here is an example:

```
data class Person(val firstName:String, val lastName:String)
val l = FXCollections.observableArrayList(
    Person("John","Smith"),
    Person("Linda","Gray"),
    Person("Kate","Winslow") )
val listView = ListView<Person>(l).apply{
    cellFactory =
        object : Callback<ListView<Person>,
                          ListCell<Person>> {
            override
            fun call(listView:ListView<Person>)
                :ListCell<Person> {
              return object : ListCell<Person>() {
                override
                fun updateItem(item:Person?,
                               empty:Boolean) {
                  // Must call super
                  super.updateItem(item, empty)
                  val index = this.index
                  var name:String? = null
                  // Format name
                  if (item != null && !empty) {
                    name = "" + (index + 1) + ". " +
                       item?.lastName + ", " +
                       item?.firstName
                  }
                  setText(name)
                  setGraphic(null)
```

Figure 6-1 A Simple
ListView

```
                }
              }
            }
          }
        }
}

val vb = VBox(
    listView
)
... add vb to scene ...
```

The updateItem() method is where the magic happens: you can set a text, or a graphic, or both to render the cell contents. Other than the name suggests, the setGraphic() function takes a Node as its parameter, so we can also handle objects of a higher grade of complexity here. For the preceding example, the outcome looks like shown in Figure 6-2.

The cells of a ListView can be made editable. For this aim, you basically set a

```
val converter:StringConverter<Person> = object :
    StringConverter<Person>(){
        ...
    }
val cellFactory1:Callback<ListView<Person>,
                    ListCell<Person>> =
    TextFieldListCell.forListView(converter)
```

as a cell factory, and in addition make the ListView editable:

Figure 6-2 A ListView
with Cell Renderer

```
val listView = ListView<Person>(l).apply{
    isEditable = true
    cellFactory = cellFactory1
}
```

A working example is shown in the book's source repository.

Tables with TableView

A TableView is an extremely versatile control for displaying tabular data. Among its features are

- It allows for data as a list of objects of any type or as a list of maps.
- It has built-in cell renderers for many data types, but you can define your own renderers.
- It makes editing of table data possible, either via built-in or your own cell factories.
- It allows for the user changing the column order.
- It has built-in sorting capabilities, and you can define your own sorting policies.
- It allows for selecting one or more rows.
- It automatically adds scrollbars if necessary.
- A TableView is *virtualized*, meaning it only handles the data currently visible. Because of that, a data list of thousands of entries does not impose a problem at all.
- It allows for nested columns.

With all that in mind, you can see that programming TableViews can be a challenging task. A complete coverage of all possibilities is out of scope for this book, but I at least want to give you a starting point for your own tables.

For this aim, we define a `Person` class with first and last name, the birthday, and with one of F, M, or D as gender. The table should show all properties as texts. Editing should be allowed, in which case the name parts and the gender should show up as text edit fields and the birthday as a date picker.

The class uses properties, so changes in the data model immediately reflect in the table view, and user input gets automatically transported to the model:

```
class Person {
    enum class Gender { F, M, D }
    val firstNameProperty: Property<String> =
        SimpleStringProperty()
    fun firstNameProperty() = firstNameProperty
    var firstName: String
        get() = firstNameProperty.getValue()
        set(value) { firstNameProperty.
                        setValue(value)   }
    val lastNameProperty: Property<String> =
        SimpleStringProperty()
    fun lastNameProperty() = lastNameProperty
    var lastName: String
        get() = lastNameProperty.getValue()
        set(value) { lastNameProperty.
                        setValue(value)   }
    val birthdayProperty: Property<LocalDate> =
        SimpleObjectProperty()
    fun birthdayProperty() = birthdayProperty
    var birthday: LocalDate
        get() = birthdayProperty.getValue()
        set(value) { birthdayProperty.
                        setValue(value)   }
    val genderProperty: Property<Gender> =
        SimpleObjectProperty()
    fun genderProperty() = genderProperty
    var gender: Gender
        get() = genderProperty.getValue()
        set(value) { genderProperty.
                        setValue(value)   }

    constructor(firstName:String, lastName:String,
                birthday:LocalDate, gender:Gender){
        this.firstName = firstName
        this.lastName = lastName
        this.birthday = birthday
        this.gender = gender
    }
}
```

It is also possible to use simple types instead of properties, but then we'd have to write much more plumbing code in order to bind the view to the data model.

The rest of the data model work looks simple for an example setup:

```
val l = FXCollections.observableArrayList<Person>(
    Person("Peter", "Smith",
        LocalDate.of(1988, Month.APRIL, 24),
        Person.Gender.M),
    Person("Linda", "Gray",
        LocalDate.of(1970, Month.DECEMBER, 10),
        Person.Gender.F),
```

```
        Person("Arny", "Bellevue",
            LocalDate.of(2001, Month.JANUARY, 4),
            Person.Gender.D)
)
```

Next, we have to define column properties:

```
    val firstNameColumn =
        TableColumn<Person, String>("First Name").apply{
            isEditable = true
            cellValueFactory = PropertyValueFactory(
                "firstName")
            cellFactory = personTextFieldRenderer
        }
    val lastNameColumn =
        TableColumn<Person, String>("Last Name").apply{
            isEditable = true
            cellValueFactory = PropertyValueFactory(
                "lastName")
            cellFactory = personTextFieldRenderer
        }
    val birthdayColumn =
        TableColumn<Person, LocalDate>("Birthdate").apply{
            isEditable = true
            cellValueFactory = PropertyValueFactory(
                "birthday")
            cellFactory = dateFieldRenderer
        }
    val genderColumn =
        TableColumn<Person, Person.Gender>("Gender").apply{
            isEditable = true
            cellValueFactory = PropertyValueFactory(
                "gender")
            cellFactory = genderTextFieldRenderer
        }
```

The isEditable = true makes sure that the cells are editable. The cellValueFactory settings determine the way how the table view accesses the data model. Because the data list contains objects and we use properties, the built-in PropertyValueFactory does the job.

The cellFactory assignments potentially imply more coding work, because this is the place where the conversion to the visual cell contents happens, and here also the user input gets converted to the appropriate data type. For a string to TextField mapping however, this is still easy, because the TextFieldTableCell class has a method forTableColumn<S>() that readily gives us an appropriate cell factory. Just replace the type argument S by the row data class, for example, by Person. For the gender column, we can also provide a TextField editor for input, but we have to provide a StringConverter that performs the conversion. Only for the date picker, a fully fledged implementation inheriting from TableCell is necessary. We therefore add in front of the column definition:

```
val personTextFieldRenderer =
    TextFieldTableCell.forTableColumn<Person>()

val genderTextFieldRenderer =
        TextFieldTableCell.
        forTableColumn<Person,Person.Gender>(
    object : StringConverter<Person.Gender>() {
        override fun toString(p:Person.Gender) = "[${p}]"
        override fun fromString(s:String) = s.let {
```

```
            val v = it.replace(Regex("\\W+"),"").uppercase()
            when(v) {
                "M", "F", "D" -> Person.Gender.valueOf(v)
                else -> Person.Gender.D
            }
        }
    }
)
```

```
val dateFieldRenderer =
    DatePickerTableCell.
    forTableColumn<Person>(datePickerEditable=true)
```

The full listing for class `DatePickerTableCell` reads (best placed in its own file)

```
public class DatePickerTableCell<S, T>()
        : TableCell<S, LocalDate>() {
  private var datePicker:DatePicker? = null
  private var converter:StringConverter<LocalDate>
  private var datePickerEditable = true

  init {
    this.converter = LocalDateStringConverter()
  }

  constructor(datePickerEditable:Boolean):this() {
    this.datePickerEditable = datePickerEditable
  }

  constructor(converter:StringConverter<LocalDate>)
        : this() {
    this.converter = converter
  }

  constructor(converter:StringConverter<LocalDate>,
        datePickerEditable:Boolean):this() {
    this.converter = converter
    this.datePickerEditable = datePickerEditable
  }

  override fun startEdit() {
    // Make sure the cell is editable
    if (!isEditable() || !tableView.isEditable()
        || !tableColumn.isEditable()) return

    // Let the ancestor do the plumbing job
    super.startEdit()

    // Create a DatePicker if needed, and set it as
    // the graphic
    datePicker ?: createDatePicker()
    graphic = datePicker
    text = null
  }

  override fun cancelEdit() {
    super.cancelEdit()
    text = converter.toString(item)
    graphic = null
  }
```

```
override fun updateItem(item:LocalDate?, empty:Boolean) {
  super.updateItem(item, empty)
  // The cell is being edited or not
  if (empty) {
    text = null
    graphic = null
  } else {
    if (isEditing) {
      datePicker?.setValue(item as LocalDate)
      text = null
      graphic = datePicker
    } else {
      text = converter.toString(item)
      graphic = null
    }
  }
}

private fun createDatePicker() {
  datePicker = DatePicker().apply{
      setConverter(converter)
      // Set the current value in the cell
      setValue(this@DatePickerTableCell.item
          as LocalDate)
      // DatePicker properties
      setPrefWidth(this@DatePickerTableCell.width
          - this@DatePickerTableCell.graphicTextGap * 2)
      setEditable(this@DatePickerTableCell.
                  datePickerEditable)
      // Commit the new value after any change
      valueProperty().addListener(
            object : ChangeListener<LocalDate> {
        override fun changed(
              prop:ObservableValue<out LocalDate>,
              oldValue:LocalDate, newValue:LocalDate) {
          if (this@DatePickerTableCell.isEditing) {
              text = converter.toString(newValue)
              this@DatePickerTableCell.
                  commitEdit(newValue)
          }
        }
      })
  }
}

companion object {
    fun <S> forTableColumn(...) = ...
    (left out for brevity)
}
}
```

We are now ready to construct the TableView (see Figure 6-3 for the outcome):

```
val tv = TableView(l).apply{
    placeholder = Text(
      "No visible columns and/or data exist.")
    // <- optional
    isEditable = true
    columns.addAll(
```

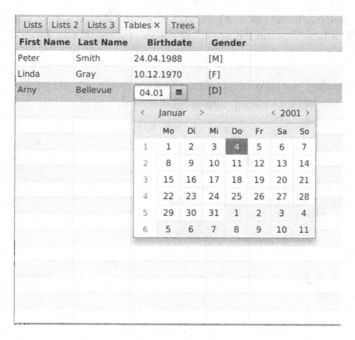

Figure 6-3 A TableView in Action

```
        firstNameColumn,
        lastNameColumn,
        birthdayColumn,
        genderColumn
    )
}
... add tv to the scene ...
```

For CSS styling table views, see the documentation at https://openjfx.io/javadoc/19/javafx. graphics/javafx/scene/doc-files/cssref.html#tableview. Also, find `modena.css` on the Web for the default styles. Here just an excerpt of selectors you can use:

– **.table-view**
  The TableView itself.
– **.table-row-cell and .table-cell**
  Point to all the cells. Use them for setting font, color, aso.
– **.table-row-cell:odd and .table-row-cell:even**
  Even and odd rows.
– **.column-header and .column-header-background**
  Point to the column header.
– **.table-view .placeholder**
  Use this to style the placeholder.

Trees with TreeView

In order to show hierarchical structured data, you can use the TreeView control. To create it, you have to stack `TreeItem` instances, either without or with children, for leaf or branch nodes, respectively.

Note There is also a TreeTableView that presents hierarchical data in a more table-like fashion. We don't talk about TreeTableViews in this book, but you can look inside the JavaFX documentation to learn more about it.

To simplify the coding, we introduce a DSL builder for TreeItem hierarchies. It is for Strings, but you should be able to adapt the code for other types if needed.

```
interface Element {
    var label:String
    fun compose(builder: TreeItem<String>)
}

abstract class Tag() : Element {
    val children = mutableListOf<Element>()
    override var label:String = ""

    protected fun <T : Element>
    initTag(tag: T, init: T.() -> Unit): T {
        tag.init()
        children.add(tag)
        return tag
    }

    override fun compose(builder: TreeItem<String>) {
        for (c in children) {
            builder.children.add(
              TreeItem<String>(c.label).
                also{ c.compose(it) }
            )
        }
    }

    fun build():TreeItem<String> =
        TreeItem<String>(label).also{ compose(it)  }
}

abstract class TagBase() : Tag() {
    fun item(label: String, init: (Item.() -> Unit)={}) {
        val a = initTag(Item(), init)
        a.label = label
    }
    // more child types...
}

class Tree : TagBase()
class Item : TagBase()

fun tree(init: Tree.() -> Unit) = Tree().also{ it.init() }
```

It is now easy to create and show tree views, as the following example depicts:

```
val tree = tree {
  item("Departments") {
    item("Sales") {
      item("Smith, John")
      item("Evans, Linda")
    }
    item("IT") {
      item("offshore") {
        item("Kalolu, Uru")
      }
```

```
            item("onshore"){
              item("Arab, Aurel")
              item("Gatter, Alina")
            }
          }
        }
      // We can perform logic inside the builder:
      // (1..3).forEach{ i ->
      //     item("Extra "+i)
      // }
    }.build()

    val tv = TreeView(tree).apply{
        setShowRoot(false)
    }
    ... add tv to scene ...
```

See Figure 6-4 to see how it looks like.

Trees can be made editable. The procedure is very similar to what we described earlier for table views, so we don't go into details on that matter for TreeViews here. Just as a primer, in order to add basic editing capabilities, you can adapt the code as follows:

```
    val tv = TreeView(tree).apply{
        setShowRoot(false)
        // Making it editable:
        isEditable = true
        cellFactory = TextFieldTreeCell.forTreeView()
    }
```

In order to style TreeViews via CSS, there are a few properties you can adapt. In order to, for example, set some basic cell properties, you can write

```
.tree-cell {
    -fx-text-fill: blue;
    -fx-font-size: 10pt;
}
.tree-cell:collapsed {
    -fx-font-weight: normal;
```

Figure 6-4 A TreeView in Action

```
}
.tree-cell:expanded {
    -fx-font-weight: bold;
}
```

Summary

In this chapter, we talked about ListView, TableView, and TreeView, three controls that show collection data on the scene. We investigated ways to address different data list item types and introduced possibilities to tailor cell rendering, including enabling editing capabilities on cells. We further handled data binding by using properties and also explained how to apply styling to those views via CSS.

Events

7

Event handling traditionally is an important topic in frontend development. This is because users often *do* something like clicking the mouse button or entering text, and the application is supposed to appropriately *react* to it. In this chapter, we talk about the way JavaFX handles events, as usual stressing Kotlin techniques for streamlining our coding.

What Events Are and Event Processing

Events are occurrences of interest, with mouse and keyboard actions being two predominant examples. In JavaFX, events get described by objects of type

```
javafx.event.Event
```

or any of its subclasses, and the instances of this type primarily expose three properties:

- **Event Source**
  The object on which the event occurred. You write `.source` to get it, as an instance of type `Any`. For example, if you click a `Rectangle` and a handler for mouse click events is installed, the rectangle is the source. As events get handed through the dispatcher chain, which is an automatically generated list of parties involved, the event source changes dynamically. For example, if you click a `Rectangle` and the rectangle is placed inside an `HBox`, and both register click handlers, for the rectangle's click handler the rectangle is the source, whereas for the container's click handler the container itself is the source.
- **Event Target**
  An event target is an object where event handling occurs. You can obtain it via `.target`, and the object returned is of class `EventTarget`. The target is internally important for creating event dispatcher chains, but unless you create your own node classes, you as an application developer won't use it too often.
- **Event Type**
  JavaFX not only uses class inheritance for distinguishing between event types but also the value you get from `.eventType` if called on the event object. Event types, represented by class `EventType`, handle event type hierarchies not via class inheritance, but instead via type parameter inheritance. So there is an `EventType< MouseEvent >`, but no `MouseEventType : EventType`.

© The Author(s), under exclusive license to APress Media, LLC, part of Springer Nature 2023
P. Späth, *Frontend Development with JavaFX and Kotlin*,
https://doi.org/10.1007/978-1-4842-9717-9_7

Immediately after the system detects an event, its processing inside JavaFX happens in two distinct phases:

- In the *capturing* phase, events get passed outside-in through the event chain, so, for example, stage scene VBox Rectangle, if clicked on the rectangle. Elements get informed about the events in that phase if they register *event filters* (not event handlers!). Inside the filters, elements are eligible to *consume* events, effectively canceling any further processing.
- In the *bubbling* phase, events get passed inside-out through the event chain, for example, click a Rectangle surrounding pane scene stage. During that phase, all event handlers (not event filters!) registered get invoked. Events can be consumed inside any handler, effectively canceling any further processing.

Note Any node in JavaFX can be involved in event handling, even if it otherwise does not provide user interactivity.

Event Handlers and Filters

In order to register event handlers for the event bubbling phase or event handlers as `event filters` for the event capturing phase, you can use one of the generic functions `addEvent-Handler()` and `addEventFilter()` on classes that are subject to event processing:

```
val rect1 = Rectangle(100.0,100.0,Color.BLUE)
.apply{
    addEventHandler(MouseEvent.MOUSE_CLICKED,
                    { mouseEvent ->
        println("Rect: " + mouseEvent.toString())
    })
}


val rect2 = VBox(
    Rectangle(100.0,100.0,Color.AQUA)
).apply{
    addEventFilter(MouseEvent.MOUSE_CLICKED,
                    { mouseEvent ->
        println("Parent: " +
            mouseEvent.toString())
        // if you want to cancel further processing
        // (the event won't make it to the rectangle):
        mouseEvent.consume()
    })
}
```

Actually, the second parameter in both function calls must be of type `EventHandler`, but since this one has just a single abstract method, often referred to as SAM, the Kotlin compiler knows how to translate the lambda function literal into the appropriate type.

Table 7.1 shows a list of some of the event types you can use for event handlers and event filters.

The `Node` class provides quite some convenience functions for adding handlers to the bubbling event processing phase. They all have the common form `onXXX(value:EventHandler)`, with XXX being one of "KeyTyped," "MouseClicked," "MouseEntered," aso. The API documentation of `Node` lists them all. Unfortunately, in this case, the Kotlin compiler cannot deduce the correct type of

Table 7.1 Event Types

CONSTANT	DESCRIPTION
Event.ANY	Common supertype for all events.
InputEvent.ANY	Common supertype for all input events.
WindowEvent.ANY	Common supertype for all window event types.
WindowEvent. WINDOW_CLOSE_REQUEST	There is an external request to close that window.
WindowEvent. WINDOW_HIDING	Occurs on a window just before it is hidden.
WindowEvent. WINDOW_HIDDEN	Occurs on a window just after it is hidden.
WindowEvent. WINDOW_SHOWING	Occurs on a window just before it is shown.
WindowEvent. WINDOW_SHOWN	This event occurs on a window just after it is shown.
ActionEvent.ANY	Common supertype for all action event types.
ActionEvent.ACTION	The only valid EventType for an ActionEvent.
KeyEvent.ANY	(Subclass of InputEvent) Common supertype for all key event types.
KeyEvent.KEY_PRESSED	(Subclass of InputEvent) A key has been pressed.
KeyEvent.KEY_RELEASED	(Subclass of InputEvent) A key has been released.
KeyEvent.KEY_TYPED	(Subclass of InputEvent) A character-generating key was typed (pressed and released).
MouseEvent.ANY	(Subclass of InputEvent) Common supertype for all mouse event types.
MouseEvent.MOUSE_CLICKED	(Subclass of InputEvent) A mouse button has been clicked (pressed and released on the same node).
MouseEvent.MOUSE_ENTERED	(Subclass of InputEvent) The mouse enters a node.
MouseEvent.MOUSE_EXITED	(Subclass of InputEvent) The mouse exits a node.
MouseEvent.MOUSE_MOVED	(Subclass of InputEvent) The mouse moves within a node and no buttons are pressed.
MouseEvent.MOUSE_PRESSED	(Subclass of InputEvent) A mouse button is pressed.
MouseEvent.MOUSE_RELEASED	(Subclass of InputEvent) A mouse button is released.
TouchEvent.ANY	(Subclass of InputEvent) Common supertype for all touch event types.
TouchEvent.TOUCH_MOVED	(Subclass of InputEvent) The touch point is moved.
TouchEvent.TOUCH_PRESSED	(Subclass of InputEvent) The touch point is pressed (touched for the first time).
TouchEvent.TOUCH_RELEASED	(Subclass of InputEvent) The touch point is released.
TouchEvent. TOUCH_STATIONARY	(Subclass of InputEvent) The touch point is pressed and still (doesn't move).

the handler, so we cannot again just use a lambda function as a parameter. Nevertheless, with a little utility function, we can elegantly use the on… family of function. Just add inside a utility file

```
fun <T : Event> EH(clos:(event:T) -> Unit):
       EventHandler<T> =
object : EventHandler<T>{ override fun handle(event:T){
    clos(event)
}}
```

Inside our coding, we can now set handlers as in

```
val rect = Rectangle(100.0,100.0,Color.PINK).apply{
    onMouseEntered = EH{ mouseEvent:MouseEvent ->
        println("Rect: " + mouseEvent.toString())
    }
}
```

Drag and Drop Procedures

In Chapter 3, we already spent some time talking about drag and drop. In this chapter, we repeat some of what we already learned there, but instead more stress the use-case perspective of that topic.

In JavaFX, three modes of drag and drop are supported:

- **Simple press-drag-release handling**
  Only one node is involved: the node on which the gesture is initiated. This mode normally gets used if you want to change the shape or position of a node.
- **Full press-drag-release handling**
  Both drag source and drop target nodes get informed by drag events. This mode is useful if a relation like "connected" or "member-of" needs to be established.
- **Drag and drop full gesture**
  Sending and receiving any kind of data, even between different applications, including non-JavaFX programs.

As an example for simple drag'n'drop, more precisely drag without drop, consider the following snippet:

```
val p1 = Pane()
val dragDelta = object{ var x=0.0; var y=0.0 }
val tf1 = TextField("Source Node").apply{
    onMousePressed = EH{
        e -> println("Source: pressed")
        dragDelta.x = layoutX - e.sceneX
        dragDelta.y = layoutY - e.sceneY
        cursor = Cursor.MOVE
    }
    onMouseDragged = EH{
        e -> println("Source: dragged")
        layoutX = e.sceneX + dragDelta.x
        layoutY = e.sceneY + dragDelta.y
    }
    onDragDetected = EH{
        e -> println("Source: dragged detected")
    }
    onMouseReleased = EH{
        e -> println("Source: released")
        cursor = Cursor.HAND
    }
}
val tf2 = TextField("Target node").apply{
    onMouseDragEntered = EH{ e ->
        println("Target: drag entered") }
    onMouseDragOver = EH{ e ->
        println("Target: drag over") }
```

```
        onMouseDragReleased = EH{ e ->
            println("Target: drag released") }
        onMouseDragExited = EH{ e ->
            println("Target: drag exited") }
    }
    tf1.layoutX = 0.0
    tf1.layoutY = 0.0
    tf2.layoutX = 200.0
    tf2.layoutY = 0.0
    p1.children.addAll(tf2, tf1)
    ... add p1 to the scene ...
```

The `dragDelta` is needed for coordinates housekeeping, to make sure the dragged node follows the mouse movement while dragging. Note that we used `Pane` as a container, such that the manual positioning during the drag movement and container layouting don't interfere with each other. A `Pane` simply does not do any layouting. If you start a program containing that snippet and try to move tf1 over tf2, the console shows

```
Source: pressed
Source: dragged [repeated]
Source: dragged detected
Source: dragged [repeated]
Source: released
```

You can see that the prospected drop node does not receive a single event in that mode.

In order to perform a "full mode" drag and drop, you add two things to the simple mode code:

1. In the `onMousePressed` handler, you invoke `setMouseTransparent( true )` on the source node. This way, it is possible that mouse events leak through to the drop target, even if the source got moved during dragging and lies on top of the target. In the `onMouseReleased` handler, you should revert that via `setMouseTransparent( false )`.
2. In the `onDragDetected` handler, you invoke `startFullDrag()`.

The following lines show an example of how to do that:

```
val p = Pane()
val dragDelta = object{ var x=0.0; var y=0.0 }
val src = TextField("Source Node").apply{
    onMousePressed = EH{ e ->
        println("Source: pressed")
        dragDelta.x = layoutX - e.sceneX
        dragDelta.y = layoutY - e.sceneY
        // Make sure the node is not picked
        setMouseTransparent(true)
        cursor = Cursor.MOVE
    }
    onMouseDragged = EH{ e ->
        println("Source: dragged")
        layoutX = e.sceneX + dragDelta.x
        layoutY = e.sceneY + dragDelta.y
    }
    onDragDetected = EH{ e ->
        println("Source: dragged detected")
        startFullDrag()
    }
    onMouseReleased = EH{ e ->
        println("Source: released")
        // Make sure the node is picked
```

```
                setMouseTransparent(false)
                cursor = Cursor.HAND
            }
        }
    val tgt = VBox( Text("Target node"),
        Rectangle(200.0,50.0,Color.LIGHTSALMON).apply{
            onMouseDragEntered = EH{ e ->
                println("Target: drag entered") }
            onMouseDragOver = EH{ e ->
                println("Target: drag over")
                fill = Color.LIGHTSALMON.darker()
            }
            onMouseDragReleased = EH{ e ->
                println("Target: drag released")
                fill = Color.LIGHTGREEN
            }
            onMouseDragExited = EH{ e ->
                println("Target: drag exited") }
        } )
    src.layoutX = 0.0
    src.layoutY = 0.0
    tgt.layoutX = 200.0
    tgt.layoutY = 0.0

    p.children.addAll(tgt, src)
    ... add p to the scene ...
```

The console now shows that the drop target reacts on drag events:

```
Source: pressed
Source: dragged [repeated]
Source: dragged detected
Source: dragged [repeated]

Target: drag entered
Target: drag over [repeated]
Source: dragged [repeated]
Target: drag released
Source: released
Target: drag exited
```

In order to start sending data via drag'n'drop *full* gesture, in the `onDragDetected` handler call `startDragAndDrop()` and as a parameter provide the configuration for the data to be sent. The call returns a `Dragboard` where you set the contents and possibly provide a visual clue. A simple example for an in-app transfer of some text is shown here:

```
    val tf1 = TextField().apply{
        promptText = "Enter something, then drag"
        onDragDetected = EH{
            e -> println("Source: dragged detected")
            if(text.isNotBlank()) {
                startDragAndDrop(
                *TransferMode.COPY_OR_MOVE).run {
                    // from now on, no more mouse events,
                    // instead drag events.
                    // "this" = Dragboard
                    setDragView(Image("/dnd.png",false),
                        0.0,0.0)
                    setContent(ClipboardContent().apply{
                        putString(text.trim()) })
```

```
                   }
                   cursor = Cursor.MOVE
               }
               e.consume()
       }
       onDragDone = EH{
           e -> println("Source: drag done")
           when(e.transferMode) {
             TransferMode.MOVE -> {
               text = "" }
             else -> {}
           }
           cursor = Cursor.TEXT
       }
}

val tf2 = TextField().apply{
    promptText = "Drop here"
    onDragOver = EH{ e ->
        // If drag board has a string, let the event
        // know that the target accepts copy and move
        // transfer modes
        e.dragboard.run {
          if(hasString()) {
            e.acceptTransferModes(
                *TransferMode.COPY_OR_MOVE)
          }
        }
        e.consume()
    }
    onDragDropped = EH{ e ->
        // Transfer the data to the target
        val txt = e.dragboard.let{ it.getString() }
        if(txt != null) text = txt
        e.setDropCompleted(txt != null) // success?
        e.consume()
    }
}
val textFieldExample = HBox(10.0, tf1, tf2)
// ... add to scene ...
```

Dragging and dropping is completely decoupled and mediated by `Dragboard`. There is no reason why you can't, for example, write a drop target accepting images from a DnD (Drag'n'Drop) initiated by an image viewer on your PC. The API documentation for `TransferMode`, `DragEvent`, and `Dragboard` tells you more; see https://openjfx.io/javadoc/19/javafx.graphics/javafx/scene/package-summary.html.

Summary

In this chapter, we talked about how to use events and apply Kotlin best practices to effectively handle them. We introduced the two event processing phases, event capturing and event bubbling, and we also implemented code for handling drag and drop in JavaFX.

Effects and Animation

8

Effects add some visual sugar to your scenes, in the sense of "make it gloomy," "add some shadow," "apply some blurring," and so on. Animation can be used for the same purpose, but depending on the functionality your application is supposed to provide, it may add a time dimension to the program. Think of computer animation or sound visualization. In this chapter, we talk about what JavaFX has to offer in these two fields.

About Effects

Effects can be applied to any `Node` and its descendants via

```
someNode.effect = someEfect
```

where `Effect` (package `javafx.scene.effect`, module `javafx.graphics`) is the common supertype of all effects. Effects often can be chained:

```
// input image -> eff1 -> eff2 -> output image
val eff1 = SomeEffect(...)
val eff2 = SomeOtherEffect(...).apply{ input = eff1 }
someNode.effect = eff2
```

The API documentation at https://openjfx.io/javadoc/19/javafx.graphics/javafx/scene/effect/package-summary.html tells you whether or not effect chaining is possible and lists up all effect-related classes.

The following list describes some of the effects available in JavaFX:

Note There is no guarantee that a particular effect is available on your hardware and platform. You have to try. In general, your application should not depend on whether effects work or not.

– **Blend**
Blends two inputs together. Possible inputs: the outcome from other effects (including color or image pixels as pseudo-effects) and the node rendered
– **Bloom**
Makes brighter portions of the input image appear to glow, based on a configurable threshold
– **BoxBlur**
Applies a simple box filter kernel, with separately configurable sizes in both dimensions, and an iteration parameter that controls the quality of the resulting blur

© The Author(s), under exclusive license to APress Media, LLC, part of Springer Nature 2023
P. Späth, *Frontend Development with JavaFX and Kotlin*,
https://doi.org/10.1007/978-1-4842-9717-9_8

- **ColorAdjust**
  Allows for a per-pixel adjustments of hue, saturation, brightness, and contrast
- **DisplacementMap**
  Shifts each pixel by a distance specified by the contents of an array-like data structure
- **DropShadow**
  Adds a drop-shadow to nodes
- **GaussianBlur**
  Applies a Gaussian blur
- **Glow**
  Makes the input image appear to glow, based on a configurable intensity threshold
- **InnerShadow**
  Renders a shadow inside the edges of the given content with the specified color, radius, and offset
- **Lighting**
  Simulates a light source shining on the given content. Gives 2D objects a three-dimensional appearance
- **MotionBlur**
  A blurring using a Gaussian convolution kernel, with a configurable radius and angle
- **PerspectiveTransform**
  Provides non-affine transformation of the input content
- **Reflection**
  Renders a reflected version of the input below the actual input content
- **SepiaTone**
  Produces a sepia tone effect, similar to antique photographs
- **Shadow**
  Creates a monochrome duplicate of an input with blurry edges

The source archive of this book provides some example use cases for effects. Figures 8-1, 8-2, and 8-3 show some examples for effects applied.

Animating Your Scenes

Animation is defined as changing the properties of a node over time. This includes position and sizing properties, but also the appearance of the node.

Five key concepts are important to understand for mastering JavaFX animations:

- **Transitions**
  A set of predefined animations that perform one of translation, scaling, rotation, gradually changing the fill color, fading in and out, and a few others. Combining transitions for sequential and parallel execution is possible, too.
- **Timeline**
  If transitions are not powerful enough for your needs, you can define a timeline that defines a progression of any set of node properties. On a timeline, you set a number of pairs of key frames and key values.
- **Key frame**
  Represents a specific instant on the timeline.

Figure 8-1 Effects Applied 1

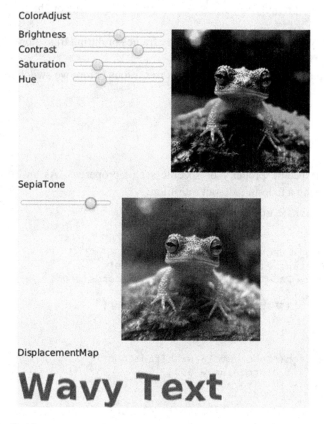

Figure 8-2 Effects Applied 2

Figure 8-3 Effects Applied 3

- **Key value**
  Represents a specific property value together with some key frame on the timeline.
- **Interpolator**
  Calculates property values *between* adjacent key frames or during transitions.

In the following paragraphs, we first talk about transitions before we switch to using timelines for animating scenes.

Transitions

Transitions act on a specific property or specific set of properties. As an example, consider the following code, showing a fade-in/fade-out transition:

```
import book.kotlinfx.util.*
...

val transiFading = HBox(5.0).apply{
  val rect = Rectangle(200.0, 50.0, Color.RED)
  val fadeInOut = FadeTransition(Duration.seconds(2.0),
                                 rect)
  val fin = Button("Fade in"){ with(fadeInOut){
      fromValue = 0.0; toValue = 1.0
      cycleCount = 1
      play() } }
  val fout = Button("Fade out"){ with(fadeInOut){
      fromValue = 1.0; toValue = 0.0
      cycleCount = 1
      play() } }
  val cycle = Button("Cycle"){ with(fadeInOut){
      fromValue = 1.0; toValue = 0.0
```

Table 8.1 Built-In Transitions

NAME	PROPERTIES AFFECTED	DESCRIPTION
FadeTransition	opacity	Fading in and out.
FillTransition	fill	Changes the fill property (as a color).
StrokeTransition	stroke	Changes the stroke (stroke must be a color).
TranslateTransition	translateX translateY translateZ	Changes the position.
RotateTransition	rotate	Changes the rotation angle.
ScaleTransition	scaleX scaleY scaleZ	Changes the scaling factor.
PathTransition	translateX translateY	Moves along a path, optionally performing rotation.
ParallelTransition	–	Runs two or more transitions in parallel.
SequentialTransition	–	Runs two or more transitions sequentially.
PauseTransition	–	Just pausing. Makes sense in a SequentialTransition chain only.

```
        cycleCount = 4; isAutoReverse = true
        play() } }

    children.addAll(fin, fout, cycle, rect)
}
// ...add transiFading to scene...
```

All transitions have such `fromXXX` and `toXXX` properties, and there is also a `byXXX` variant, not shown in the example, for specifying a transition property difference instead of an absolute target. The code also shows a *cycle* mode for repeated transitions, optionally with `isAutoReverse = true` if you want to have the transition direction reversed for every other cycle. The API documentation shows you more, but in order to give you an overview, Table 8.1 lists all the built-in transitions.

It is somewhat challenging to build your own transitions – you basically have to provide an implementation for the abstract `Transition` class (package `javafx.animation`). The sources of the built-in transitions should give you a starting point (press F3 in Eclipse or CTRL+B in IntelliJ IDEA, the cursor over the class name, to see the sources).

Timeline Animations

In case you prefer a more storyboard-like setup for creating animations, or if transitions are not flexible enough for your needs, you can use timelines and key-frame and key-value pairs. At a bare minimum, you need one property you want to change, one key-frame/key-value pair for the beginning of an animation, and another one for the end, as the following example shows:

```
val msg = Text("JavaFX animation at work!").apply{
    textOrigin = VPos.TOP
    font = Font.font(24.0)
}

// Initial and final key frames
val initKeyValue = KeyValue(msg.translateXProperty(),
    0.0)
val initFrame = KeyFrame(Duration.ZERO,
    initKeyValue)
val endKeyValue = KeyValue(msg.translateXProperty(),
    100.0)
```

```
val endFrame = KeyFrame(Duration.seconds(3.0),
    endKeyValue)

Timeline(initFrame, endFrame).apply{
    cycleCount = Timeline.INDEFINITE // run forever
}.also{
    it.play() // immediately start
}

// ...add msg to the scene...
```

You can add more key frames to the constructor of `Timeline`, if needed.

The `Animation` class, a superclass of `Timeline`, contains a couple of methods, namely, `start()`, `stop()`, `pause()`, and others you can use to control an animation. You can, for example, place buttons for triggering those methods into a toolbar. Via `.rate = ...`, again an accessor in class `Timeline`, you can adjust the playback speed.

Normally, the transition of the property values *between* adjacent key frames happens in a linear fashion, but you can change that behavior by adding instances of class `Interpolator` to the constructor of `KeyValue`:

```
...
val keyValue = KeyValue(msg.translateXProperty(),
    100.0, Interpolator.EASE_IN)
...
```

This snippet uses one of the predefined interpolators from class `Interpolator`. If you need a custom interpolator, you can create one via

```
val myInterpolator = object : Interpolator() {
  override
  fun curve(timeFraction:Double):Double {
      return ... some calculation ...
      // e.g.,   return 1.0*timeFraction
      // makes a linear interpolator
  }
}
```

Both the parameter and the return value of `curve()` are doubles from range $0.0 \ldots 1.0$. As an easy accelerating interpolator, use `return timeFraction * timeFraction`, and for a decelerating one, you could write `return Math.sqrt( timeFraction )`.

Summary

In this chapter, we talked about effects and animation for adding sugar to your scenes, either via nonfunctional visual enhancements or via entering the time domain in the form of transitions or timelines.

Concurrency

9

For a good user experience mark, you are well advised to immediately react on any user input. For example, if you run a snippet with a button and text field bound together like shown here:

```kotlin
import book.kotlinfx.util.*
...
val tf = TextField()
val btn = Button("Click me"){
    Thread.sleep(5000)
    tf.text = "Setting at " + LocalTime.now()
}
val vb = VBox(5.0, btn, tf)
    .apply{ style="-fx-padding:10;" }
// ...add vb to scene...
```

the UI freezes for five seconds after you click the button, making it irresponsive to any user input. Apart from the *quick and dirty* remedy

```kotlin
    val btn = Button("Click me"){
        Thread{
            Thread.sleep(5000)
            tf.text = "Setting at " + LocalTime.now()
            // Or better, because UI changes should
            // _always_ be performed in JavaFX' UI
            // thread:
            //      Platform.runLater{
            //          tf.text = "Setting at " +
            //                      LocalTime.now()
            //      }
        }.start()
    }
```

for background execution, there are other, presumably better, ways to handle concurrency, and we talk about some possibilities in this chapter.

The JavaFX Concurrency Framework

JavaFX provides a small, but quite useful, collection of classes and interfaces under the umbrella of the javafx.concurrent package. Figure 9-1 shows an overview.

© The Author(s), under exclusive license to APress Media, LLC, part of Springer Nature 2023
P. Späth, *Frontend Development with JavaFX and Kotlin*,
https://doi.org/10.1007/978-1-4842-9717-9_9

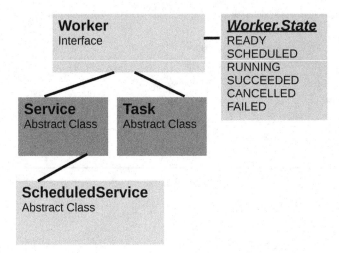

Figure 9-1 The JavaFX Concurrency Framework

On top of the class hierarchy, you find the `Worker` interface. It introduces state housekeeping and declares a couple of properties eligible to be bound to UI Node properties. You normally don't provide implementations of `Worker` in your application; instead, you inherit from subclasses of `Worker`, namely, `Task` and `Service`, which already implement most of the boilerplate code needed for JavaFX background processing. A few concepts defined in `Worker` however are worth mentioning:

- A Worker has a well-defined life cycle. Starting from `Worker.State.READY`, state transitions walk through `Worker.State.SCHEDULED`, `Worker.State.RUNNING`, and in the end one of `Worker.State.SUCCEEDED` or `Worker.State.FAILED`.
- There are three properties that can be used to monitor a Worker's progress: `totalWork`, `workDone`, and `progress`. The latter one, `progress`, is supposed to return −1 or a number between 0.0 and 1.0. You often use this one to monitor the overall progress of a background task.
- Only if in the RUNNING state, `progress` lies in the range [0.0, 1.0]. Otherwise, set it to −1.
- If the Worker completes normally, the result of the Worker will be set as the `value` property.
- The `value` property's type corresponds to the Worker's generic type parameter.

For all the other details, you can consult the API documentation at https://openjfx.io/javadoc/19/javafx.graphics/javafx/concurrent/package-summary.html.

The first implementation of `Worker` we talk about is `Task` from package `javafx.concurrent`. You use it for one-shot running some background task. It can provide an outcome value when its work is done, and the type of the result returned must be specified as a generic type argument while constructing `Task`. If you don't need such a return value, you can use `Unit`. As a bare minimum, you must implement the `call()` method:

```
val tsk = object : Task<Unit>() {
    override fun call() {
        ...
    }
}
-- or --
val tsk = object : Task<Int>() {
    override fun call():Int {
        ...
        return 42
```

```
        }
    }
```

In the following example, we use a task to just sleep for a while. As a progress indicator, we bind the `progress` property to a slider and also use the `message` property to present some state information on the UI:

```kotlin
import book.kotlinfx.util.*
...

fun main(args:Array<String>) {
    Application.launch(App::class.java, *args)
}

class App : Application() {
    val closeListeners = mutableListOf<()->Unit>()

    override
    fun start(primaryStage:Stage) {
        ...
        primaryStage.addEventHandler(
            WindowEvent.WINDOW_CLOSE_REQUEST,
            { closeListeners.forEach{ it() } })
        ...
    }

    private fun contents():Node {
        val pool = Executors.newFixedThreadPool(10).also{
            pool ->
            // shut down pool on window close request,
            // otherwise the app won't exit.
            closeListeners.add( pool::shutdownNow )
        }
        val sl = Slider(0.0,1.0,0.0)
        val txt = Text()
        val btn = Button("Click me"){
            val tsk = object : Task<Unit>() {
                override fun call() {
                    updateMessage("Started")
                    for(i in 0 until 1000) {
                        if(isCanceled) break
                        try{ Thread.sleep(10) }
                        catch(e:InterruptedException){
                            break}
                        updateProgress(i.toDouble(),1000.0)
                    }
                    updateMessage("Done")
                }
            }
            sl.valueProperty().bind(tsk.progressProperty())
            txt.textProperty().bind(tsk.messageProperty())
            pool.submit(tsk)
        }

        return VBox(5.0,
            btn, tf,
            HBox(4.0, btn2, sl2, txt2)
        ).apply{ style="-fx-padding:10;" }
    }
}
```

Because we use a thread pool for running the background task, and the application won't exit if the thread pool is not shut down, we install an appropriate window-close listener performing that job. In addition, regularly checking the cancellation state via `.isCanceled` and acting accordingly is important for the task properly functioning. Catching the `InterruptedException` for `Thread.sleep()` serves the same purpose. Only then a task can be canceled from outside, for example, triggered by a button click. The `updateProgress()` and `updateMessage()` call transport status information to the outer world. Here, we bind them to a slider and a text node, respectively.

In order to export intermediate values, inside the `call()` method you would write

```
updateValue(42)   // or whatever generic type is used
```

You can then use the task's `valueProperty()` in the surrounding code to work intermediate results (or, of course, the final result returned by `call()` after the task finishes).

In case you need a reusable background processing component, you must use an instance of the `Service` class (package `javafx.concurrent`) instead. It is basically a wrapper around `Task`, and in order to use it, you must implement the `Task` generator method `createTask()`:

```
val srvc = object : Service<Unit>() {
    override fun createTask() =
        object : Task<Unit>() {
            override fun call() {
                ...
            }
        }
}
```

This way, the `Service` class knows how to create a new `Task` whenever needed. To start the background processing, all you then have to do is `srvc.start()`. The `Service` class maintains its own thread pool, so we don't have to take care of that in our code as was the case for using tasks without `Service`.

The preceding slider example rewritten for a `Service` class implementation is as follows:

```
import book.kotlinfx.util.*
...

    val sl = Slider(0.0,1.0,0.0)
    val txt = Text()
    val srvc = object : Service<Unit>() {
        override fun createTask() =
            object : Task<Unit>() {
                override fun call() {
                    updateMessage("Started")
                    for(i in 0 until 1000) {
                        if(isCanceled) break
                        try{ Thread.sleep(10) }catch(
                            e:InterruptedException){break}
                        updateProgress(i.toDouble(),1000.0)
                    }
                    updateMessage("Done")
                }
            }.also{
                sl.valueProperty().bind(
                    it.progressProperty())
                txt.textProperty().bind(
                    it.messageProperty())
            }
        override fun canceled() { unbindAll() }
        override fun failed() { unbindAll() }
```

```
          override fun succeeded() { unbindAll() }
          private fun unbindAll() {
              sl.valueProperty().unbind()
              txt.textProperty().unbind() }
      }
  val btn = Button("Start Service"){
      if(srvc.state == Worker.State.READY)
          srvc.start()
  }
  val btnCancel = Button("Reset"){
      srvc.cancel()
      srvc.reset()
      sl.value = 0.0
      txt.text = ""
  }

  val hb = HBox(4.0, btn, btnCancel, sl, txt)
  ...add hb to scene...
```

You can see that after `cancel()` you can rewind the service via `reset()`. The unbinding of the slider and text node makes sure we can freely adjust them if the service is not in RUNNING state.

The `ScheduledService` is an extension of `Service`. Its purpose is to provide a service that automatically restarts once done. The API documentation tells you more about this class.

About Kotlin Coroutines for JavaFX

Kotlin coroutines introduce a new concurrent programming paradigm, by favoring nonpreemptive concurrency over setting up a thread-related architecture. We cannot possibly handle Kotlin coroutines thoroughly in this chapter, though. The topic, albeit fascinating, is just too big, and mastering all aspects of it is just an all too challenging task. But I at least want to give you a starting point if you want to start mixing JavaFX and coroutine concepts in your application.

As a preparational step, add the following dependencies to your project:

```
dependencies {
  implementation project(':Ch00_Util')
  implementation 'org.jetbrains.kotlinx:'+
      'kotlinx-coroutines-javafx:1.7.2'
  ...
}
```

The "kotlinx-coroutines-javafx" artifact simplifies adding coroutines to a JavaFX project. This is helpful, because JavaFX heavily depends on separating the main (GUI) thread from auxiliary background processing threads, while coroutines try to abstract away multithreading pitfalls that make a developer's life hard if using threads.

We start with providing a simple console-like view. We could have used the STDOUT stream for the same purpose, but it is actually easy to achieve in JavaFX, so we can just as well create a UI component and keep things together:

```
  val listData = FXCollections.
      observableArrayList("","","","")
  suspend fun pushMsg(s:String){ with(listData){
      add(0,s); if(size>4) removeAt(4)} }

  val lv = ListView<String>(listData)
  ...later, add lv to scene...
```

This little console shows four lines, and you can call pushMsg() to insert lines, newest on top. Because of the suspend modifier, this function can only be called from inside coroutine scopes or other suspend functions.

The first example shows how to run everything in the JavaFX main UI thread. In

```
import kotlinx.coroutines.javafx.JavaFx as Main
import book.kotlinfx.util.*
...
    val btn1 = Button("Countdown") {
        val job = GlobalScope.launch(
                Dispatchers.Main) { // main UI thread
            for (i in 10 downTo 1) {          // countdown
                pushMsg("Countdown $i ...") // show text
                delay(500L)                  // wait 0.5s
            }
            pushMsg("Done!")
        }
        userData = job // make accessible from outside
    }
    val btn2 = Button("←Stop") {
        (btn1.userData as Job).cancel() }

    ...add btn1 and btn2 to scene...
```

the GlobalScope.launch( ) with Dispatchers.Main as argument makes sure that the lambda runs in the main UI thread, so it can update the UI. The "Main" here is just a rewritten "JavaFx" by virtue of the corresponding import statement. Other than you might guess from the delay(500) statement, the code does *not* block the UI. This is because a delay( ) is conceptionally different from a Thread.sleep( ), as the former temporarily gives away the program flow, letting the UI do other work. This technique is called *structural concurrency*, because things do not actually run in parallel, but by means of language and library constructs interleave with each other, in the end leading to a fluently reacting UI.

Once in a while however, real parallel background processing is needed. Consider, for example, heavy CPU-intensive calculations triggered by a UI action like a button press. As an example, consider a PI calculator that deliberately only slowly converges, just to make our point clear:

$$\pi = 4 \cdot \left(\frac{1}{1} - \frac{1}{3} + \frac{1}{5} - \frac{1}{7} + \cdots \right)$$

An algorithm for this is readily written:

```
fun stupidPi():Double {
  var i = 1L
  var sgn = 1
  var v = 0.0
  while(i < 10_000_000_000){
    v += 4.0 * sgn/( 2.0*i.toDouble() - 1.0 )
    sgn *= -1; i++
  }
  return v
}
```

If you add this to a button press action listener, the UI freezes for a long time. To improve this, first of all we make this a suspending function by prepending suspend:

```
suspend fun stupidPi() {
  ... same as above ...
}
```

For now, this is just a marker – there is nothing inside which can communicate concurrently with the outer world. In order to send it to the background now, we can use a non-UI `Dispatcher`:

```
import kotlinx.coroutines.javafx.JavaFx as Main
import book.kotlinfx.util.*
...
    suspend fun stupidPi() {
      ... same as above ...
    }
    val btn = Button("Calculate PI"){
        GlobalScope.launch(Dispatchers.Default) {
          val pi = stupidPi()
          Platform.runLater {
            pushMsg(pi.toString())
          }
        }
    }
```

Now the calculation does no longer block the UI. Not bad, but there are a couple of caveats with this code. First of all, there is no way to cancel the calculation while it is running. Next, the calculator is rather quiet and does not tell about its progress. And in addition, we kind of need to know beforehand how many iterations need to be run to achieve a satisfactory result. We can handle all this the classic way by adding stops to the calculator loop and observing cancel variables and all that stuff, but it would be nice if we could instead

- Make the calculator UI-agnostic, for example, by letting it send intermediate calculation results to some pipe, without having to know what happens with these data.
- Remove the upper limit in the calculator loop and write `while ( true )` instead. We would appreciate if we didn't have to add too much boilerplate code to handle cancellation.
- Handle the communication between the background calculator thread and the main UI thread in a more transparent way.

All these can be achieved by using *coroutine producers*. Although this technology is marked *experimental*, it is already stable enough to be used without having to expect major changes in the API. Consider the following code:

```
import kotlinx.coroutines.javafx.JavaFx as Main
import book.kotlinfx.util.*
...
    val btn1 = Button("Calculate PI"){
        // run using background threads
        suspend fun CoroutineScope.stupidPi() =
              produce<Double>(Dispatchers.Default) {
          var i = 1L
          var sgn = 1
          var v = 0.0
          while(true){
            v += 4.0 * sgn/( 2.0*i.toDouble() - 1.0)
            sgn *= -1; i++
            if(i%100_000_000 == 0L) send(v)
          }
        }
        val job = GlobalScope.launch(Dispatchers.Main) {
          // launch coroutine in the main UI thread
          val producer = stupidPi()
          while(true) {
            pushMsg(producer.receive().toString())
```

```
        }
      }
      userData = job
  }
  val btn2 = Button("←Stop"){
      (btn1.userData as Job).cancel() }

  ...add btn1 and btn2 to scene...
```

You can see that the calculator just emits double values once in a while, representing intermediate calculation results in a producer pipe. Besides, it seems to run indefinitely, but in fact the `send()` call knows how to break the loop gracefully if needed. On the receiver side, there is another `while ( true )` loop that by virtue of the `.receive()` knows how to stop iterating if `Job.cancel()` gets called. Also, the send-receive pair performs the plumbing between the UI and the background process, such that a `Platform.runLater` no longer is needed.

The result of this is a fluently, in parallel running calculation that seamlessly interacts with the UI.

Summary

In this chapter, we talked about concurrency in JavaFX, focusing on the JavaFX concurrency framework and Kotlin coroutines. Concerning the latter, we showed how to use structural concurrency to avoid having to use background threads and how to perform real parallel processing in cases where CPU-intensive calculations are necessary.

Index